ELEMENTARY LOGIC

ELEMENTARY LOGIC

Revised Edition

WILLARD VAN ORMAN QUINE

HARVARD UNIVERSITY PRESS

CAMBRIDGE, MASSACHUSETTS

LONDON, ENGLAND

Library of Congress Catalog Card Number: 80-81978

ISBN 978-0-674-24451-1

PREFACE, 1980

PUBLISHERS' SAMPLES of fifty-five logic textbooks have accumulated in my office, all introductory and in English. Quantification theory, or the first-order predicate calculus, is covered in one way or another in most of them. Forty years ago it was covered in none. In my elementary one-semester course I was resolved to impart at least that vital minimum of modern lore, along with the mandatory traditional material; and no text existed to the purpose. My *Mathematical Logic* had just come out, but it was too technical. I wanted a method which, though precise and deductively complete, could be quickly learned and easily applied. I devised what I could at the time and made a small book of it in six weeks as an emergency measure. It was published by Ginn and Company in 1941 as *Elementary Logic*. I used it for the formal part of my semester courses, supplementing it with one or another traditional logic textbook for traditional themes.

It differed much from the little book that is now before us. When Ginn let it go out of print, I was content to acquiesce; for I had meanwhile arrived at alternative techniques that were more to my liking, and had just written *Methods of Logic*. Likewise I demurred years later when other publishers asked to reprint *Elementary Logic*. However, it was their expression of interest that set me to thinking of a revised edition. *Methods of Logic* afforded full sustenance for an intensive semester course or more; *Elementary Logic* could still be useful as affording just a brief logical component in a semester course dealing also with other matters, possibly philosophy or English composition or computer programming.

In 1965 Harper and Row brought out the revised edition in paperback and Harvard University Press in hard cover. Harper and Row has now discontinued the paperback and Harvard, to my gratification, has taken it up.

In an adjoining preface it is remarked that the proof procedure used for quantification theory in this edition came from an appendix to *Methods of Logic*. That was an appendix of 1955 to an accidentally

v

delayed second edition of *Methods* (1959). It was devoted to showing, after Gödel, that quantification theory admits of a complete proof procedure; and the argument went through with unprecedented ease when applied to this particular proof procedure. Since it is also an easy proof procedure to explain, justify, and use, I revived it for the revised *Elementary Logic.* More recently I elevated it also to the status of "main method" in the third edition of *Methods,* and used it there as the basis on which to justify a sheaf of alternative procedures. The two books have progressed thus alternately in a pedestrian sort of way, like feet. The present one remains as it was in 1965, however, except for the addition of this preface.

W.V.Q.

Boston, March 1980

PREFACE TO THE REVISED EDITION

THIS LITTLE book provides a single strand of simple techniques for the central business of modern logic, seldom looking to the right or to the left for alternative methods or peripheral problems. Basic formal concepts are explained, the paraphrasing of words into symbols is treated at some length, a testing procedure is given for truth-function logic, and a complete proof procedure is given for the logic of quantifiers. At the end there are brief glimpses of further matters. The book is meant as a convenient encapsulation of minimum essentials. Students might use it who need a bit of logic as a prerequisite for some other subject, or in preparation for a general qualifying examination, or as part of a survey course. The book is for readers who would spare themselves the breadth of coverage afforded by my *Methods of Logic*, not to mention advanced works.

This edition, appearing after twenty-four years, is much revised. Fully a third is new. There is some change of notation, much updating of terminology, and a nearly complete turnover in crucial techniques of testing and proving. Some of what was novel in the first edition, and is here superseded, had a certain appeal: the extrication techniques, perhaps, and the singularity transformation. Other devices are favored here as being more customary and no less efficient.

The testing procedure used here for truth-function logic is the time-honored method of alternational and conjunctional normal form. The proof technique used here for quantification theory is one that was noted in (V) of the Appendix of *Methods of Logic:* a matter simply of proving the inconsistency of one or more prenex schemata by instantiating until a truth-functional inconsistency is accumulated. When ease of inculcation, ease of justification, and ease of application are added together and averaged out, it is far and away the easiest proof technique for quantification theory that I know. It derives from the tradition of Skolem and Herbrand.

vii

The Introduction and Chapter I are unchanged except for negligible emendations. Chapter II is little changed in its first seven sections, §§14–20, except terminologically; "compositional" becomes "truth-functional," "frame" becomes "schema," "statement variable" becomes "letter." The rest of old Chapter II, viz. §§21–30, gives way now to §§21–27, whereof two thirds is new writing and one third is drawn from the old pages. Chapter III carries over unchanged except for adjustment of section numbers, restoration of parentheses in connection with quantifiers, revision of the end of what is now §36, and modernization of terminology in what is now §30. Chapter IV continues easily recognizable only through the first four of its original fifteen sections. These four are already conspicuously modified by changes of terminology (here "stencil" becomes "predicate") and occasional further revisions. The rest of the chapter, old §§46–56, gives way now to new §§43–48, which echo the old only in occasional paragraphs.

Readers acquainted with *Methods of Logic* will find reminders of that book in some of the examples. But these things have not been borrowed from there. They were in the 1941 edition of *Elementary Logic* and were borrowed thence for *Methods of Logic* with acknowledgment in 1950.

Those readers and others will wonder, when they get to p. 108, at my defining validity as truth under all substitutions; for they know that the validity of a quantificational schema consists in its being fulfilled by all classes and relations. Truth under all substitutions looks wrong on two counts. The scope of "all substitutions," unlike that of "all classes and relations," varies with the resources of one's vocabulary; and even if those resources are great, there will, by a theorem of Cantor's, be classes and relations in excess of what can be portrayed in substitutions. The fact is, though, that if our vocabulary of available substitutions includes the notations of elementary number theory, any quantificational schema that is true under all substitutions will also be fulfilled by all classes and relations. This follows from Hilbert and Bernays, *Grundlagen der Mathematik*, vol. 2, pp. 234–253, and it is why I can define validity as I do on p. 108. I am happy to, for it makes for a shorter story. Advanced students should know both accounts, of course, and why they agree.

W. V. Q.

Harvard, Massachusetts
August 1965

PREFACE TO THE 1941 EDITION

MODERN LOGIC is not purely an outgrowth of the traditional formal logic. Problems in the foundations of mathematics have been an independent source of motivation. But the general student who looks into modern logic is usually in search merely of techniques and analyses which accomplish, more thoroughly and on a wider scale, the sort of work for which the traditional logic was designed. Accordingly much of the subtle machinery which he encounters proves irrelevant to his purposes.

Authors of current introductory texts recognize the necessity of dodging those mathematically motivated subtleties. In so doing, however, they usually err in the opposite direction, neglecting the very techniques wherein modern logic has chiefly surpassed traditional logic even from a non-mathematical point of view. What is most neglected is quantification theory—the theory of 'some', 'every', 'no', and pronouns. Introductory texts tend to terminate in the so-called class algebra, which is a trifling fragment of quantification theory, scarcely more inclusive than the traditional syllogistic. Yet the idioms analyzed and manipulated in quantification theory play so basic a role in all discourse that a working command of the main lines of the theory should surely be an aim of any beginning logic course. In Chapter IV of this book I have tried to meet the difficulty by reworking quantification theory for general elementary purposes.

Chapter II deals with the simpler part of logical theory, viz., the theory of statement composition. The novelties of the present approach are no less considerable in this department than in quantification theory. In both departments the fundamental method turns on progressive transformation of expressions into equivalents, rather than on deductive chains. The general approach is more akin to the algebraic practice of putting equals for equals than to the geometrical practice of deducing theorems from axioms.

The purpose of the book has been to give a better understanding of the basic logical constructions and reasonings involved in ordinary discourse. Accordingly nearly half the book, comprising Chapters I and III, has been devoted to analyzing verbal idioms. Though the analysis proceeds by translation into a schematic symbolism, the symbolic machinery has been kept to a minimum. Instead, e.g., of adopting four logical symbols corresponding to the four connectives 'if . . . then', 'or', 'and', and 'not', as is usual in 'symbolic logic', we get along with symbols corresponding to just the latter two. Mutually equivalent but dissimilar statements of ordinary language consequently tend to coalesce on translation into symbols, whereas in the usual 'symbolic logic' such statements more often receive dissimilar symbolic translations which have afterwards to be proved equivalent by symbolic methods. Thus much of what usually goes into symbolic machinery is transferred, under the present procedure, to the interpretative side of logic. This course is prompted by an inclination to work directly with ordinary language until there is a clear gain in departing from it.

For the historical background, the reader is referred to the numerous small-print passages in my recent *Mathematical Logic*. Thus I may dispense, in the present book, with most of what would otherwise need to be said by way of allocating credit to predecessors. But in addition I am indebted to Dr. John C. Cooley, who helped me give the elementary logic course at Harvard in 1938–1940. and issued several mimeographed editions of an *Outline of Formal Logic* for use as a text in that course. I have followed him in applying the terms 'equivalence', 'validity', and 'implication' primarily to frames [= schemata], and in formulating these notions by reference to instances. The general attitude that I adopt toward frames (§ 14) is due largely to him, but is traceable also in part to an unpublished paper on variables by Mr. Albert Wohlstetter (M.A. thesis in philosophy, Columbia University, 1938). To Dr. Carl G. Hempel I am grateful for helpful suggestions.

Cambridge, January 1941   W. V. Q.

CONTENTS

III · QUANTIFICATION

IV · QUANTIFICATIONAL INFERENCE

ELEMENTARY LOGIC

§ 1. Introduction

THE SCOPE of the term 'logic' has varied widely from writer to writer through the centuries. But these varying scopes seem all to enclose a common part: the logic which is commonly described, vaguely, as the science of necessary inference. There is a growing tendency to limit the term 'logic' to this field; and it is in conformity with this tendency that the term is used in the present book.

A somewhat less vague characterization of the field is as follows. Certain basic locutions, to begin with, including 'if', 'then', 'and', 'or', 'not', 'unless', 'some', 'all', 'every', 'any', 'it', etc., may be called *logical*. They appear in statements on any and every subject. The pattern according to which the other more special ingredients of a statement are knit together by these basic locutions may be called the *logical structure* of the statement. For example, the statements:

(1)   Every microbe is an animal or a vegetable,

(2)   Every Genevan is a Calvinist or a Catholic,

have the same logical structure. Now logic studies the bearing of logical structure upon truth and falsehood.

A statement is *logically true* if it is true by virtue solely of its logical structure; i.e., if all other statements having that same structure are, regardless of their subject matter, likewise true. A simple example is:

Every microbe is either an animal or not an animal.

Two statements are *logically equivalent* if they agree in point of truth or falsehood by virtue solely of their logical structure; i.e., if no uniform revision of the extralogical ingredients of the statements is capable of making one of the statements true and one false. The statement:

1

If something is neither animal nor vegetable, it is not a microbe,

for example, is logically equivalent to (1). One statement *logically implies* another if from the truth of the one we can infer the truth of the other by virtue solely of the logical structure of the two statements. The statement:

Every Genevan is a Calvinist,

thus, logically implies (2).

Logical truth, equivalence, and implication are not always as readily detected as they are in the case of the above examples. Even at the level of simplicity of these examples error may occasionally arise. We might be tempted, for example, to regard (1) as logically implying:

(3)   Some animals are microbes,

whereas this idea can be seen to be wrong by changing 'microbe' to 'azalea' and observing that (1) remains true while (3) becomes false. Perhaps the reader was prevented by ordinary good sense from falling into this simple error; but he may be assured nevertheless that there are more and more complicated cases, without end, where logical truth and equivalence and implication are hidden from all men save those who have special techniques at their disposal. Logic is concerned with developing such techniques.

A partial development of logic, in this sense of the term, stems from Aristotle and has been known traditionally as 'formal logic'. But the past century brought radical revisions of concepts and extensions of method; and in this way the confined and stereotyped formal logic of tradition has come to be succeeded by a vigorous new science of logic, far surpassing the old in scope and subtlety. The traditional formal logic is not repudiated, not refuted, but its work is done more efficiently by the new logic as an incidental part of a larger work.

Logic, in its modern form, may conveniently be treated as falling into three parts. In the theory of *truth functions,* first, we study just those logical structures which emerge in the construction of compound statements from simple statements by means of the particles 'and', 'or', 'not', 'unless', 'if . . . then', etc. In the theory of *quantification,* next, we study more complex structures, wherein the aforementioned particles are mingled with generalizing particles such as 'all', 'any', 'some', 'none'. In the theory of *membership,* finally, we turn to certain special structures involved in discourse about universals, or abstract objects. This trichotomy afforded the basic plan of my larger work *Mathematical Logic*.

But there is equal justice in an alternative classification, whereby logic proper is taken as comprising just the first two of those three parts, while the theory of membership is placed outside logic and regarded as the basic extralogical branch of mathematics.[1] Whether we construe 'logic' in the tripartite way or in this narrower bipartite way is a question merely of how far we choose to extend the catalogue of 'logical locutions' alluded to earlier. According to the wider version, logic comes to include mathematics;[2] according to the narrower version, a boundary survives between logic and mathematics at a place which fits pretty well with traditional usages.

The scope of the present book, in any case, is substantially those first two parts—truth functions and quantification. This bipartite province may be called 'elementary logic' or simply 'logic' at the reader's discretion. Far narrower than logic in the tripartite sense of *Mathematical Logic,* it stops short of all topics of a distinctly mathematical flavor; it adheres to matters which no one would hesitate to classify as logical. Still it far outruns the traditional formal logic.

The matters here treated are subject not only to the described dichotomy between statement composition and quantification, but also to a second dichotomy of another sort which runs across the first. For, antecedent to the task of investigating isolated logical structures in their relation to truth and falsehood, logic has also the task of isolating those structures. This is a task of analyzing ordinary statements, making implicit ingredients explicit, and reducing the wholes to systematically manipulable form. It is the interpretative task, as opposed to the calculative. The intersection of these two dichotomies divides the book into four chapters.

[1] Cf. § 48; also *Mathematical Logic*, pp. 127–28. For this point of view I am indebted to Prof. Alfred Tarski.

[2] Cf. *Mathematical Logic*, pp. 5, 126, 237–79.

I · STATEMENT COMPOSITION

§ 2. Truth Values

STATEMENTS ARE sentences, but not all sentences are statements. Statements comprise just those sentences which are true and those which are false. These two properties of statements, truth and falsity, are called *truth values;* thus the truth value of a statement is said to be truth or falsity according as the statement is true or false.

The sentences 'What time is it?', 'Shut the door', 'Oh, that I were young again!' etc., being neither true nor false, are not counted as statements. Only declarative sentences are statements. But closer examination reveals that by no means all declarative sentences are statements. The declarative sentence 'I am ill' is intrinsically neither true nor false; it may simultaneously be uttered as true by one person and as false by another. Similarly the sentence 'He is ill' is intrinsically neither true nor false, for the reference of 'he' varies with the context; in one context 'He is ill' might properly be uttered as true, and in another as false. Indeed, the sentence 'Jones is ill' presents the same difficulty; for in the absence of context it is not clear whether 'Jones' refers to Henry Jones of Lee St., Tulsa, or John J. Jones of Wenham, Mass. The sentence 'It is drafty here' may be simultaneously true for one speaker and false for a neighboring speaker; and 'Tibet is remote' is true in Boston and false in Darjeeling. The sentence 'Spinach is good', if uttered in the sense 'I like spinach' rather than 'Spinach is vitaminous', is true for a few speakers and false for the rest.

The words 'I', 'he', 'Jones', 'here', 'remote', and 'good' have the effect, in these examples, of allowing the truth value of a sentence to vary with the speaker or scene or context. Words which have this effect must be supplanted by unambiguous words or phrases before we can accept a declarative sentence as a statement. It is

5

only under such revision that a sentence may, as a single sentence in its own right, be said to have a truth value.

Such adjustments suffice to prevent a statement from being *simultaneously* true in one mouth or context and false in another. Even after such adjustments have been made, however, the truth value of a statement would still seem frequently to vary with time. The sentence:

(1)   Henry Jones of Lee St., Tulsa, is ill

is true at one time and false at another, concomitantly with Jones's variations in health. Again 'The Nazis annexed Bohemia' was false before 1939 and is now true, whereas 'The Nazis will annex Bohemia' was true before 1939 and is now false—unless that annexation is destined to be undone and repeated.

But logical analysis is facilitated by requiring rather that each *statement* be true once and for all or false once and for all, independently of time. This can be effected by rendering verbs tenseless and then resorting to explicit chronological descriptions when need arises for distinctions of time. The sentence 'The Nazis will annex Bohemia', uttered as true on May 9, 1936, corresponds to the statement 'The Nazis annex [tenseless] Bohemia after May 9, 1936'; and this statement is true once and for all regardless of date of utterance. The shorter statement 'The Nazis annex Bohemia', construed tenselessly, affirms merely that there is at least one date, past, present, or future, on which such annexation takes place; and this statement again is true once and for all. The sentence (1) above, uttered as a tensed sentence on July 28, 1940, corresponds to the *statement* 'Henry Jones of Lee St., Tulsa, is [tenseless] ill on July 28, 1940'; on the other hand, the *statement* (1), construed tenselessly, might be accounted true once and for all on the grounds that Jones has had or will have at least one illness in his life.

Whereas these refinements are important as a theoretical basis of analysis, it will be convenient in the practical construction of examples to use as statements such sentences as 'Jones is ill', or even 'You will hear from me'. But we are to imagine, always, that each such sentence is expanded into one or another appropriate full statement. The methods of technical analysis will be fashioned in conformity with the understanding that a statement is a sentence which is uniformly true or uniformly false independently of context, speaker, and time and place of utterance.

By means of the connectives 'and', 'or', 'if . . . then', 'neither

. . . nor', etc. we combine simple statements to form compound statements; and the truth value of the compound statement depends in one way or another upon the truth values of the components. The compound statement:

(2)   Jones is ill and Smith is away,

for example, is true just in case both of the component statements 'Jones is ill' and 'Smith is away' are true. The compound:

(3)   Neither is Jones ill nor is Smith away

is true just in case neither of the components is true. The compound:

(4)   Jones is ill or Smith is away

is true just in case the one component or the other is true. There may also be various sorts of interdependence between the truth value of one compound and the truth value of another compound; it is obvious, for example, that the compounds (2) and (3) will not both be true, nor will (3) and (4).

By successive application of these statement connectives we can build up more and more elaborate statements:

(5)   If Jones is ill or Smith is away then neither will the Argus deal be concluded nor will the directors meet and declare a dividend unless Robinson comes to his senses and takes matters into his own hands.

The truth value of such a statement is determined still by the truth value of the components. The truth value of (5) can be decided once we know the truth value of the seven components:

(6)   Jones is ill,

(7)   Smith is away,

(8)   The Argus deal will be concluded,

(9)   The directors will meet,

(10)   The directors will declare a dividend,

(11)   Robinson will come to his senses,

(12)   Robinson will take matters into his own hands.

Such discovery of the truth value of the compound from the truth values of the components is increasingly difficult, however, for increasingly elaborate compounds; and it thus becomes necessary to develop a systematic technique for the purpose (§ 22). Techniques likewise become necessary for tracing out relationships of interdependence between the truth value of one elaborate compound and the truth value of another. Modern logic, at its most elementary level, is concerned with the development of such techniques. We shall address ourselves to these problems in chapter II. In the present chapter, meanwhile, we must familiarize ourselves with the subject matter by casting an eye over some of the commonest modes of statement composition.

Exercise

Which of the following sentences are statements, in the strict sense of the present section? How might the others be elaborated so as to become statements?

> Iron is a metal.
>
> Iron is a vegetable.
>
> Stromboli resumed activity in 1937 and has not stopped yet.
>
> Washington died before Lincoln was born.
>
> Whenever I travel more than a hundred miles from here, I get homesick.
>
> The doctor was a classmate of Anthony Eden's.

§ 3. Conjunction

In the symbolism of modern logic the dot '.' is used instead of the statement connective 'and'; thus §2(2)[1] becomes:

(1)   Jones is ill . Smith is away.

Again the compound 'Some are born great, some achieve greatness, and some have greatness thrust upon them', i.e. 'Some are born great and some achieve greatness and some have greatness thrust upon them', becomes:

[1] The reference '§2(2)' is intended to indicate the expression which was marked '(2)' in § 2.

(2)   Some are born great . some achieve greatness . some have
         greatness thrust upon them.

Composition of two or more statements by '.' in this fashion is
known to logicians as *conjunction;* and the compound is called a
conjunction of its components.

A conjunction is true just in case all the statements whereof it
is a conjunction are individually true. A conjunction is false just in
case one or more of those component statements is false. Obviously
the order in which the component statements are written is immaterial to the truth value of a conjunction. The example from
Shakespeare could have been rendered equivalently as 'Some achieve
greatness, some have greatness thrust upon them, and some are born
great', or again as 'Some have greatness thrust upon them, some are
born great, and some achieve greatness', or in any of three other
orders. Commonly we are prompted to write a conjunction in one
order rather than another by rhetorical considerations—considerations of emphasis, climax, euphony, etc.; but such considerations
have nothing to do with truth and falsehood.

The connective 'and' is used in ordinary discourse not only between statements but between other sentences and even between
nouns, verbs, adverbs, prepositions, and other parts of speech. It is
to the use of '.' between statements that the logical term 'conjunction' applies. But the use of 'and' between nouns, verbs, or other
parts of speech is commonly only an abbreviation for the conjunctive use of 'and' between statements; thus 'Americans may enter
Canada and Mexico without passports' is short for the conjunction
'Americans may enter Canada without passports and Americans
may enter Mexico without passports'. Similarly 'Robinson comes to
his senses and takes matters into his own hands' was treated in § 2
as short for 'Robinson comes to his senses and Robinson takes
matters into his own hands'.

The conjunction formed from the two statements:

(3)   Some are born great,

(4)   Some achieve greatness . some have greatness thrust upon
         them

is not distinguishable, in our notation, from the conjunction formed
from the different pair of statements:

(5)   Some are born great . some achieve greatness,

(6)   Some have greatness thrust upon them;

nor is either of these conjunctions distinguishable from the conjunction which is formed simultaneously from the three statements (3) and

(7)   Some achieve greatness

and (6). All three of these constructions yield the same result, viz. (2). There is no damaging ambiguity in this, for it is readily seen that the truth value of (2) remains the same regardless of what choice we make among the three above interpretations; and with any other example the case is similar. If we construe (2) as a threefold conjunction of (3), (7), and (6), we must regard (2) as true just in case each of (3), (7), and (6) is true. If on the other hand we construe (2) as the conjunction of (5) and (6), we must regard (2) as true just in case (5) and (6) are both true; but the conjunction (5) is in turn true just in case its components (3) and (7) are both true, so we end again by regarding (2) as true just in case (3), (7), and (6) are true. The same result is seen to ensue when we construe (2) as the conjunction of (3) and (4). We can thus think of (2) as *at once* the conjunction of (3) and (4), the conjunction of (5) and (6), and the conjunction of (3), (7), and (6); these are the same statement (2).

We have seen that the conjunction of (3) and (4) is at the same time a conjunction of the statements (3), (7), and (6), none of which is a conjunction in turn. Similarly, in general, a conjunction of any set of statements some or all of which are conjunctions is at the same time a conjunction of another set of statements none of which are conjunctions. But we can continue to explain a conjunction of any given set of statements as true if and only if each statement of the set is true, regardless of whether the given set is the set which is free from conjunctions; thus we have seen that (2) is true if and only if (3) and (4) are true, *also* if and only if (5) and (6) are true, and *also* if and only if (3), (7), and (6) are true.

Exercise

Express this symbolically as a conjunction of three statements:

Rome and Paris are in Italy and Campione is in Switzerland.

Not having heard of Campione, can you tell whether the conjunction is true or false?

§ 4. Denial

Given any statement, we can form another by *denying* the first. The resulting *denial* is false or true according as the original statement is true or false. The denial of a statement will be written by putting the statement in question in the blank of '~(   )'; but the parentheses will be suppressed unless the statement within them is a conjunction. Thus the denial of 'Kansas touches Iowa' is:

(1)   ~ Kansas touches Iowa,

and the denial of §3(1) is:

(2)   ~(Jones is ill . Smith is away).

The tilde '~' is a modified 'n' and is conveniently read 'not'.

The method of forming the denial in ordinary language is irregular. Sometimes 'not' or 'does not' or 'fails to' is applied to the main verb; thus (1) might appear in words as 'Kansas does not touch Iowa', or 'Kansas fails to touch Iowa'. If the statement has no one main verb, denial is accomplished by one or another periphrasis; e.g., the denial (2) might be rendered in words thus:

(3)   It is not the case that Jones is ill and Smith is away.

Many other cases receive special treatment under ordinary usage. For example, '~ some are born great' would appear in words as 'None is born great', and '~ Jones is never ill' as 'Jones is sometimes ill'. A considerable simplification is therefore achieved by adopting the prefix '~' as a uniform notation of denial. This prefix might be explained as answering to the phrase 'it is not the case that', as in (3); for prefixture of this phrase does regularly have the effect of denying a statement.

The use of parentheses, to enclose a denied conjunction as in (2), is necessary in order to prevent confusing the denial of a conjunction with a conjunction whose first part is a denial. Deletion of parentheses from (2) in the fashion:

(4)   ~ Jones is ill . Smith is away

would effect a drastic change in the meaning; for (2) is the denial of §3(1), while (4) is rather the conjunction of '~ Jones is ill' with 'Smith is away'. The denial (2) holds whenever §3(1) is false, hence whenever one or both of 'Jones is ill' and 'Smith is away' are false;

on the other hand, the conjunction (4) holds only in the single case where 'Jones is ill' is false and 'Smith is away' true. (2) has the verbal equivalent (3), while (4) is equivalent rather to:

Jones is not ill but Smith is away.

Whereas conjunction combines statements two or more at a time, denial applies to statements one at a time. Statements can be denied jointly, however, by denying them severally and conjoining the denials; e.g., the statements 'Jones is ill' and 'Smith is away' can be denied jointly in the fashion:

(5) $\sim$ Jones is ill . $\sim$ Smith is away,

in words:

Jones is not ill and Smith is not away,

or more idiomatically:

(6)   Neither is Jones ill nor is Smith away.

The conjunction (5) is true just in case each of the individual denials is true (cf. § 3) and hence just in case 'Jones is ill' and 'Smith is away' are both false; thus (5) must be carefully distinguished from (2), which is true whenever *one or both* of 'Jones is ill' and 'Smith is away' are false. Falsehood merely of 'Jones is ill' is enough to verify (2), but not enough to verify (5).

After the manner of (5) we can form the joint denial not merely of two statements, but of as many as we like. Thus the conjunction:

(7) $\sim$ Jones came . $\sim$ Smith stayed . $\sim$ Robinson left,

in words:

(8)   Neither did Jones come nor did Smith stay nor did Robinson leave,

is true just in case 'Jones came', 'Smith stayed', and 'Robinson left' are all false. It must be distinguished from:

$\sim$(Jones came . Smith stayed . Robinson left),

which is true whenever one or more of 'Jones came', 'Smith stayed', and 'Robinson left' are false.

Exercise

Translate each of these into as idiomatic English as possible:

$\sim$(the train left late . $\sim$ the train arrived late).

12

$\sim$ the train left late . $\sim$ the train arrived late.

$\sim$ the train often arrives late.

$\sim$ most trains arrive late.

§ 5. 'Or'

The connective 'or' or 'either . . . or', in its most usual sense, yields a statement which is false just in case the corresponding 'neither . . . nor' statement is true. So construed, the statement:

Either Jones is ill or Smith is away

or more briefly:

(1)   Jones is ill or Smith is away

is false just in case §4(6) is true—hence just in case the parts:

(2)   Jones is ill,   Smith is away

are both false. (1) is true whenever one or both of the parts (2) are true. The method of translating (1) into terms of '.' and '$\sim$' is thus apparent; (1) can be rendered as the denial of §4(6) and hence as the denial:

(3) $\sim$($\sim$ Jones is ill . $\sim$ Smith is away)

of §4(5). Similarly the statement:

(4)   Jones came or Smith stayed or Robinson left

(with 'either' prefixed at will) becomes construed as the denial of §4(8), and hence as the denial:

(5) $\sim$($\sim$ Jones came . $\sim$ Smith stayed . $\sim$ Robinson left)

of §4(7). It is true whenever one or more of 'Jones came', 'Smith stayed', and 'Robinson left' are true; and it is false just in case these three parts are all false.

But the connective under consideration is actually subject, in ordinary discourse, to conflicting usages. The usage set forth above gives 'or' its so-called *inclusive* sense, according to which the compound is true whenever *one or more* of the components are true; but 'or' is sometimes used rather in a so-called *exclusive* sense, according to which the compound is true only in case exactly one of the components is true. Under the inclusive sense (1) is reckoned false

13

in just one case, as observed: the case where the parts (2) are both false, i.e. where §4(5) is true. Under the exclusive sense, on the other hand, (1) is reckoned false both in that case and in a further one: the case where the parts (2) are both true, i.e. where §3(1) is true. Thus, whereas (1) in the inclusive sense holds whenever §4(5) is false, on the other hand (1) in the exclusive holds if and only if §3(1) and §4(5) are both false. Whereas (1) in the inclusive sense amounts simply to the denial of §4(5), viz. (3), on the other hand (1) in the exclusive sense amounts rather to the *joint* denial of §3(1) and §4(5), viz.:

(6) ∼(Jones is ill . Smith is away) .

∼(∼ Jones is ill . ∼ Smith is away).

Similarly, whereas (4) in the inclusive sense amounted to (5), in the exclusive sense it amounts rather to:

∼(Jones came . Smith stayed) . ∼(Jones came . Robinson left) . ∼(Smith stayed . Robinson left) . ∼(∼Jones came . ∼ Smith stayed . ∼ Robinson left).

The ambiguity of 'or' is commonly resolved, in ordinary usage, by adding the words 'or both' or 'but not both'. Thus the inclusive sense of (1), viz. (3), is expressible in the unambiguous fashion:

Jones is ill or Smith is away or both;

and the exclusive sense of (1), viz. (6), is expressible in the unambiguous fashion:

(7) Jones is ill or Smith is away, but not both.

The inclusive sense of 'or' is perhaps the commoner of the two. "If a witness guesses that the steering gear was loose or the driver was drunk, and it turns out that the steering gear was loose and the driver was drunk, we do not regard the witness as mistaken. . . . At the same time the prevalent use of the expressions 'or both' and 'and/or' is a presumption in favor of the exclusive interpretation [of 'or'], since otherwise these expressions would always be superfluous."[1] But it will be convenient hereafter, in analyzing statements, to agree that 'or' is always to be understood in the inclusive sense if there is no explicit indication to the contrary. Thus (1) will be understood in the sense (3); and when the exclusive sense (6) is

[1] *Mathematical Logic,* p. 12.

intended instead of (3), we shall insist on use of the explicit wording (7) rather than (1).

Like 'and' (cf. § 3), the connectives 'or' and 'neither . . . nor' are used in ordinary discourse not only for joining statements but also for joining nouns, verbs, adverbs, etc. Those further uses are not directly relevant to our present study of statement composition; but commonly, as noted in the case of 'and,' such use of the connectives serves merely to abbreviate their use as statement connectives.

Exercises

1. Suppose we know that the statements (2) are not both true. If I then affirm (1), must I intend 'or' in the exclusive sense? And if I deny (1), must I intend 'or' in the inclusive sense? Or does our assumed knowledge make for indifference between the two senses?

2. Suppose we know rather that the statements (2) *are* both true. If I then affirm (1), must I intend 'or' in the inclusive sense? And if I deny (1), must I intend 'or' in the exclusive sense? Is anyone likely, with the assumed knowledge, either to affirm or to deny (1)? Defend your answers.

§ 6. 'But,' 'although,' 'unless'

In §§ 4–5 we have seen how three statement connectives, viz. 'neither . . . nor', the inclusive 'or', and the exclusive 'or . . . but not both', can be paraphrased in terms of 'and' and 'not' ('.', '~'). Those three statement connectives are thus seen to be theoretically superfluous; whatever can be accomplished with them can be accomplished with just conjunction and denial. Now these three connectives are by no means the only ones which are eliminable in favor of conjunction and denial. Further examples, readily dealt with, are 'but' and 'although'.

These words, as connectives of statements, are directly replaceable by 'and.' The compound:

(1)   Jones is here but Smith is ill

or again:

15

(2)   Jones is here although Smith is ill

amounts simply to:

(3)   Jones is here and Smith is ill.

The statements (1) and (2) hold under precisely the same circumstances under which (3) holds: they hold when the parts 'Jones is here' and 'Smith is ill' are both true, and fail otherwise. When one chooses 'but' or 'although' in favor of 'and', it is only for rhetorical purposes; 'but' is ordinarily used to emphasize a contrast, and 'although' is used when the contrast attains such proportions as to cause surprise. The mere contrast between being here and being away in the sick-room would lead us to use 'but' in (1); but if Jones usually sits at Smith's bedside in times of illness, we are likely to favor 'although' as in (2). Choice between 'and', 'but', and 'although' is indifferent to the truth value of the resulting statement, and resembles thus the choice of order in conjunction (cf. § 3); choice in this matter is guided, as it so often is in that, by rhetorical considerations. The only differences of meaning which are relevant to logic are those which affect the truth value of a statement; and for purposes of logical analysis 'but' and 'although' can therefore be abandoned in favor of 'and'.

Another of the connectives which prove to be eliminable in favor of conjunction and denial is 'unless'. Consider the statement:

(4)   Smith will sell unless he hears from you.

This is verified in case Smith hears from you and does not sell; it is also verified in case he fails to hear from you and then sells; and it is falsified in case he fails to hear from you and yet does not sell. (4) thus affirms that one of two things will happen: either Smith will hear from you or he will sell. But what of the case where both things happen—where he hears from you and still sells (perhaps, indeed, having heard from you that he should sell)? Should we regard (4) as rendered true by these circumstances? If so, then 'unless' amounts to the inclusive 'or'; (4) is true whenever one or both of its components are true, and false just in case both components are false. If, on the other hand, we regard (4) as falsified where Smith hears from you and still sells, then 'unless' amounts to the exclusive 'or'; (4) is true just in case one and only one of the components is true. Anyone who construes 'unless' in this fashion would in practice probably elaborate (4) in the fashion 'unless he hears from you to the contrary'.

16

'Unless' thus seems to answer to 'or'; and it seems even to share the ambiguity of 'or', as between the inclusive and the exclusive sense. In either sense, 'unless' can be eliminated in favor of conjunction and denial; for we have seen (§ 5) how to eliminate 'or' in either of its senses. But in practising with examples it will be convenient, as in the case of 'or' (cf. § 5), to dodge the existing ambiguity of usage by agreeing in general to understand 'unless' in the inclusive sense.

Between 'unless' and 'or' there is doubtless a rhetorical difference, such as was observed between 'but' and 'and'. Perhaps we tend to prefer 'unless' to 'or' when we feel that the first of the two component statements deserves more emphasis than the second, or that the first component is more likely to be true than the second. Also there is a tendency to use 'unless' where the component statements are future in tense. Note incidentally that there is a minor grammatical difference between 'unless' and 'or' as applied to futures; if, for example, we were to put 'or' for 'unless' in (4), we should have to change 'hears' to 'will hear.' In logical analysis, however, it is simplest to sweep away any special problems of tense by pretending that differences of time are recorded solely through explicit mention of epochs (cf. § 2).

Exercise

Under what circumstances would it seem natural to supplant the 'or' in:

He is at his desk or he is eating lunch

by 'unless'? by 'but'? by 'although'?

§ 7. 'If'

When Toby says:

(1)   If Hawkshaw saw me then the jig is up,

he does not thereby affirm that the jig is up. He does not regard himself as mistaken if it turns out that Hawkshaw did not see him

and the jig is not up. But he cheerfully acknowledges error if he
finds that Hawkshaw saw him and the jig is still not up. The statement (1) commits him only to the extent of ruling out the joint
truth of 'Hawkshaw saw me' and 'The jig is not up'; it records his
disbelief in the conjunction:

(2)   Hawkshaw saw me . ~ the jig is up.

Instead of affirming (1), then, he could accomplish the same result
simply by denying (2), thus:

(3)   ~(Hawkshaw saw me . ~ the jig is up).

The statement connective 'if . . . then' is in this way dispensable in
favor of conjunction and denial.

Toby's belief that (1) is true—in other words, that (2) is false—
might theoretically be grounded in any of three ways: he might
believe simply that Hawkshaw did not see him, for this is enough to
falsify the conjunction (2); or he might believe simply that the jig
is up, for this again is enough to falsify (2); or, third, he might have
no conviction on either of those points, but believe only in some
causal connection or general law whereby Hawkshaw's glimpse of
him would tend to render the jig up. Actually, however, neither the
first nor the second of these three situations provides a likely motive
for affirming (1); for in the first situation Toby could save breath
and at the same time convey more information by saying simply
'Hawkshaw did not see me,' and in the second situation he could
gain the same advantages by saying simply 'The jig is up.' A conditional, i.e., a statement of the 'if . . . then' form, is thus ordinarily affirmed only in situations of the third kind. It is ordinarily
affirmed only in ignorance of the truth values of its components.

This circumstance has led some writers to object to translating
conditionals into the form exemplified by (3); it is held that the conditional connotes some causal or psychological connection between
its components, while its translation of the form (3) connotes no
such connection. But this objection has little force, since there is no
more motive for affirming (3) than for affirming (1) where we are in
position to affirm or deny a single component outright. (3), like (1),
would in practice be affirmed only on the basis of a believed causal
connection or other general law. In (1) and (3) alike, some such
connection will normally enter into the *motivation* of the statement.
If it turns out that Hawkshaw saw Toby without recognizing him,
and if it happens further that Toby's jig is up because of a quite

extraneous matter of income-tax evasion, Toby's statement (1) remains true by coincidence; he happens merely to have uttered a true statement on mistaken grounds.

The 'then' of 'if . . . then' is of course superfluous, like the 'either' of 'either . . . or' (cf. § 5); thus (1) could be rendered equivalently and perhaps more idiomatically as:

(4)   If Hawkshaw saw me, the jig is up.

Moreover, the order in a conditional is immaterial so long as 'if' is prefixed always to the same component; thus (4) is equivalent to:

(5)   The jig is up if Hawkshaw saw me

but not to:

(6)   If the jig is up, Hawkshaw saw me.

The prefix 'only if' is the reverse of 'if'; attachment of 'only if' to one component is equivalent to attaching 'if' to the other component. For example, the compound:

(7)   The jig is up only if Hawkshaw saw me

is not equivalent to (5) but rather to (6). Whereas (5) rules out the one case (2), on the other hand (7) rules out the one case:

(8)   the jig is up . $\sim$ Hawkshaw saw me.

Sometimes the connectives 'if' and 'only if' occur together in the fashion:

(9)   The jig is up if and only if Hawkshaw saw me,

which is of course short for the conjunction of (5) and (7). Since (5) amounts to the denial (3) of (2), and (7) amounts correspondingly to the denial of (8), we can put (9) into symbols thus:

$$\sim(\text{Hawkshaw saw me} . \sim \text{the jig is up}) .$$
$$\sim(\text{the jig is up} . \sim \text{Hawkshaw saw me}).$$

This conjunction rules out the two cases (2) and (8)—hence just the two cases where 'Hawkshaw saw me' and 'the jig is up' differ from each other in point of truth value. Thus (9) is true just in case its two components are alike in truth value—both true or both false. Whereas 'and' combines statements to form a compound which is true just in case both components are true, and 'or' combines them to form a compound which is false just in case both components are false, the complex connective 'if and only if' combines them to form a compound which is true just in case the components agree in truth value.

It should be noted that there are a number of locutions which, merely for the sake of variety, are commonly used in place of 'if'. Perhaps the commonest are 'in case' and 'provided that'. Furthermore, the locution 'just in case' is synonymous with the complex connective 'if and only if'.

Exercise

Put the statement:

(i)   ∼(∼ Manordale is a good investment .

                                        ∼ Jones missed his guess)

into words using 'if . . . then'; again using 'only if'; again using 'unless'; again using 'or'; and again using 'neither . . . nor.'

Hint. To arrive at the first two translations you will have to think of one or another of the denials in (i) as a single unit, corresponding *in toto* to one of the components of (1) or (7).

§ 8. General and Subjunctive Conditionals

The remarks of § 7 must not be allowed to obscure the fact that the conditional form is used also in expressing general laws, e.g.:

(1)   If anything interests me, then it bores George.

The intimate connection between interesting me and boring George figures not merely in the motivation of (1), as § 7 might suggest, but in the content of (1); (1) indeed directly affirms such a connection.

The point is that the present example (1), which may be called a *general* conditional, differs fundamentally from §7(1) and is not a pure conditional in the sense of § 7. Its nature is more clearly exhibited in the phrasing:

(2)   Whatever may be selected, if it interests me, then it bores
           George.

This statement has the effect of affirming not one but an unlimited array of conditionals of the form:

           If . . . interests me, then . . . bores George.

20

Each of these separate conditionals, for example:

If hockey interests me, then hockey bores George,

can still be construed in the manner of § 7:

~(hockey interests me . ~hockey bores George).

The connection between interesting me and boring George is conveyed in (2) not simply by the 'if . . . then' construction, but by this in combination with the generality prefix 'whatever may be selected'. The latter device will be studied subsequently (§§ 34–35) under the head of *quantification.*

Another use of 'if' which departs radically from that considered in § 7 is exemplified by the statement:

(3)   If Hoover were now President, America would be at war.

The component sentences here are rendered in the subjunctive mood. Whereas the ordinary conditional in the indicative mood tends to be used only in ignorance of the truth or falsehood of the components (cf. § 7), subjunctive conditionals such as (3) are used only where the first component is definitely believed to be false. If we were to analyze (3) along the lines of § 7, we should have to construe the whole trivially as true in view merely of the falsehood of 'Hoover is now President' ('now' being understood of course as 'in 1940'). This analysis, however, is untenable; the truth of (3) is indeed capable of being vigorously debated as a political theory, and the knowledge that Hoover is not President and America is not at war is of no avail in settling the debate.

The methods of statement composition studied in §§ 3–7 are *truth-functional,* in the sense that the truth value of the compound depends only on the truth values of the components. Replacement of a component by another statement of like truth value does not affect the truth value of the compound. But the subjunctive conditional as of (3) is not truth-functional; the truth values of the components leave the truth value of the compound undecided. To establish the truth or falsehood of (3) we would disregard the well-known truth values of 'Hoover is now President' and 'America is at war', and proceed rather to examine various political documents, observe historical analogies, and discover relevant causal laws of a political or economic kind.

In § 7 we saw that the indicative conditional can always be construed truth-functionally, viz. as false just in case its 'if'-component is true and its 'then'-component false, even though its affirmation will ordinarily be motivated by considerations of causal connection; but in the case of the subjunctive conditional the very truth value of the whole comes to depend on such connections, the conditional being true or false according as such connections do or do not obtain.

This anomalous departure from the truth-functional sort of statement composition might indeed be dismissed on the ground that sentences in the subjunctive mood are not *statements* (cf. § 2) and hence that their union by 'if' as in (3) is not a case of *statement* composition at all. But on the other side it can be argued that such dismissal is only a grammatical quibble, and that (3) can justly be regarded as a compound of the statements 'Hoover is (in 1940) President' and 'America is at war.' It can be argued that the method of statement composition here consists not merely in applying 'if,' but in applying 'if' and switching the verbs to the subjunctive mood.

Exercises

1. Rephrase each of the following as a general conditional:

(i)   Men are mortal.
(ii)   God helps those who help themselves.
(iii)   All the world loves a lover.

Corresponding to each of these general conditionals, cite some ordinary conditional (as of § 7) which falls under it.

2. The idioms illustrated in (i)–(iii) are all equivalent to the general conditional. How many more such idioms can you think of?

§ 9. 'Because,' 'hence,' 'that'

In any case there *are* statement connectives which are not truth-functional and yet apply to genuine statements in the indicative mood. One such is 'because'. The statement:

(1)   Jones needs quinine because he has malaria

requires for its truth that the two components 'Jones needs quinine' and 'Jones has malaria' be true; but it requires something more also,

22

viz. the truth of a related general law (cf. § 8). Some results of joining true statements by 'because' are true, and some are false; truth
of a 'because' compound requires not only truth of the components
but also some sort of causal connection between the matters which
the two components describe.

Other connectives which can be used in the same sense as 'because' are 'for' and 'since'; and one which has the same sense in
reverse order is 'and hence'. We could render (1) equivalently as:

(2)   Jones has malaria and hence he needs quinine.

This version has the virtue of separating out the truth-functional
ingredient. With 'hence' omitted, (2) requires for its truth the mere
truth of 'Jones has malaria' and 'Jones needs quinine'; and the insertion of 'hence' then adds the non-truth-functional demand for a
causal connection.

This added non-truth-functional ingredient which distinguishes
'and hence' or 'because' from 'and' differs fundamentally from the
merely rhetorical ingredient which distinguishes 'but' or 'although'
from 'and' (cf. § 6). Use of 'but' or 'although' in place of 'and' may
increase or diminish the naturalness of a statement, but can never
change the truth value; on the other hand, use of 'and hence' or
'because' in place of 'and' can turn a truth into a falsehood.

The word 'that' is another departure from the truth-functional
type. This word gives rise to compounds whose truth values vary
independently of the truth values of the component statements. The
statements:

Jones believes that Paris is in France,
Jones believes that Punakha is in Bhutan,

may be respectively true and false even though the components
'Paris is in France' and 'Punakha is in Bhutan' are both true; and
the statements:

Jones believes that Punakha is in Nepal,
Jones believes that Paris is in Japan,

may be respectively true and false even though the components
'Punakha is in Nepal' and 'Paris is in Japan' are both false. Similar
results obtain when 'believes' is supplanted by 'doubts', 'says',
'denies', 'regrets', 'is surprised', etc.

Nowhere in the whole structure of standard logic are the non-
truth-functional sorts of statement composition systematically ana-

lyzed. Nowhere are general techniques developed for determining truth values of non-truth-functional compounds of statements. Each individual example tends rather to present individual problems and to call for individual treatment. In each separate case, the analysis consists in elimination: in showing how the purposes served by the given non-truth-functional statement compound could have been served just as well by means of truth-functional statement compounds plus further devices which fall outside the domain of statement composition altogether (e.g. the general conditional of § 8, or the implication of §§ 26–27, 43, 46, below). It is to be hoped that every useful statement compound of non-truth-functional kind is eliminable in one or another such fashion; though the precise manner of elimination is bound to vary not only from compound to compound but also from one context to another and from one practical situation to another. The rigor and precision of a science is indeed measured, in part, by the extent to which its formulations are free from statement compounds of non-truth-functional kinds. The theoretical elimination of such compounds from the whole of pure mathematics has long since been accomplished.

With this much by way of general comment, let us take leave of non-truth-functional statement composition. Any appreciable progress there would presuppose much in the way of cutting new trails and surmounting old obstacles—obstacles as considerable, indeed, as the philosophical problem of cause.

Exercise

Construct an 'and' compound which is true but becomes false when 'and' is changed to 'because'. Construct another which remains true when 'and' is changed to 'because', but becomes false when 'and' is changed to 'and hence'.

§ 10. Reduction to Conjunction and Denial

The truth-functional modes of statement composition thus far considered (§§ 3–7) have been seen to admit of being paraphrased in terms exclusively of conjunction and denial. The same is in fact true of all possible truth-functional modes of statement composition. So long as a statement is built up of component statements in truth-functional fashion—so long, in other words, as the replacement of any component by another statement of like truth value does not affect the truth value of the compound—we can translate the whole into an equivalent statement which is built up of the components in question by means solely of conjunction and denial.[1] We can therefore look upon conjunction and denial as the sole basic truth-functional devices; and we can require, preparatory to any logical analysis of a truth-functional compound, that the compound be first paraphrased in terms of those two basic devices. The advantage is that in devising the techniques promised in § 2 we shall then need to consider only conjunction and denial.

Given any compound built up of its components by repeated use of 'and', 'not', 'or', 'if . . . then', 'unless', etc., we have only to paraphrase each of these connectives individually as prescrbed in §§ 3–7; eventually all give way to the '.' of conjunction and the '∼' of denial. Consider, for example, the complex case §2(5). If we abbreviate the seven components §2(6)–(12) as 'J', 'S', 'A', 'M', 'D', 'C', and 'T', then §2(5) is:

(1)   If J or S then neither A nor M and D unless C and T.

But we decided in § 7 that a compound of the form 'if p then q' ('p' and 'q' being replaced by any statements) is to be paraphrased as '∼$(p . ∼q)$'. Thus (1), which is of the form 'if p then q', becomes:

(2)   ∼(J or S . ∼ neither A nor M and D unless C and T).

The elimination of 'or', next, is accomplished by § 5, according to which 'J or S' gives way to '∼(∼J . ∼S)'.

(3)   ∼(∼(∼J . ∼S) . ∼ neither A nor M and D unless C and T).

Now the remaining verbal expression has the form 'p unless q', where 'p' answers to 'neither A nor M and D' and 'q' answers to 'C and T'. But 'p unless q', according to § 6, receives the same expansion as 'p or q'—viz. '∼(∼p . ∼q)' (if we adopt the inclusive sense). Thus (3) becomes:

(4)   ∼(∼(∼J . ∼S) .
            ∼∼(∼ neither A nor M and D . ∼ C and T)).[2]

[1] Cf. *Mathematical Logic*, §§ 8–9.
[2] Note that the last occurrence of '∼' here governs 'C and T' as a whole, and not just 'C'. This point will be taken up again in § 13.

Now 'neither p nor q' gives way, according to § 4, to '$\sim p$. $\sim q$'; thus 'neither A nor M and D' becomes '$\sim$A . $\sim$ M and D'.

(5) $\sim(\sim(\sim J . \sim S) . \sim\sim(\sim(\sim A . \sim M \text{ and } D) . \sim C \text{ and } T))$.

Note that the conjunction '$\sim$A . $\sim$ M and D' had to receive a pair of parentheses in (5); for the conjunction occurs subject to a denial sign, and parentheses regularly form part of the denial notation as applied to conjunctions (cf. § 4). Finally 'M and D' and 'C and T' are to be rendered as symbolic conjunctions 'M . D' and 'C . T'; and these again must be provided with parentheses because they occur subject to denial signs. The translation of (1) into terms of '.' and '$\sim$' is thus complete:

(6) $\sim(\sim(\sim J . \sim S) . \sim\sim(\sim(\sim A . \sim(M . D)) . \sim(C . T)))$.

Exercise

In passing from (3) to (4), we construed 'unless' in the inclusive sense. If instead we were to adopt the exclusive sense, what results should we get in place of (4)–(6)?

§ 11. Grouping

A great advantage of our technical notation as of §10(6), in comparison with ordinary language as of §10(1) or §2(5), is the systematic and unambiguous manner in which grouping is indicated by parentheses. The faultiness of ordinary language in this regard is well illustrated by the phrase 'pretty little girls' camp'; this admits of the three interpretations:

> pretty (little (girls' camp)),
> pretty ((little girls') camp),
> (pretty (little girls')) camp,

and, if we allow 'pretty' to take on the sense of 'rather,' two more:

> (pretty little)(girls' camp),
> ((pretty little) girls') camp.

In paraphrasing an elaborate compound such as §10(1) we have at nearly every step to make a decision about grouping. In passing from §10(4) to §10(5), for example. we had to decide whether to construe:

(1)   neither A nor M and D

as having been formed from 'A' and 'M and D' by means of 'neither . . . nor' or as having been formed rather from 'neither A nor M' and 'D' by means of 'and'. The two versions are by no means equivalent. According to the first version, (1) is true in case 'A' and 'M and D' are both false—hence whenever 'A' and at least one of 'M' and 'D' are false. According to the second version, on the other hand, (1) is true just in case 'neither A nor M' and 'D' are both true— hence just in case 'A' and 'M' are both false and 'D' is true. According to the first version, (1) becomes '$\sim$A . $\sim$(M . D)'; according to the second version it becomes rather the tripartite conjunction '$\sim$ A . $\sim$ M . D'.

Actually the first of the two versions was chosen in paraphrasing §10(4) as §10(5). The choice was not made arbitrarily, but on the basis of a conspicuous clue: in the wording of the original §2(5) the parts 'M' and 'D' occur telescoped in the clause 'nor will the directors meet and declare a dividend', and hence obviously belong together as a conjunction governed *in toto* by 'nor'.

A similar decision had to be made in passing from §10(3) to §10(4); we had to decide whether to construe:

(2)   neither A nor M and D unless C and T

as formed from (1) and 'C and T' by means of 'unless', or as formed rather from 'A' and 'M and D unless C and T' by 'neither . . . nor'. The question is whether the clause following 'unless' in §2(5) is to be regarded as limiting everything from 'then' onward or just the part from 'nor' onward. Such a choice can be properly made only by reading the original statement sympathetically and making a conjecture as to the most likely intentions of the supposed speaker. Insofar as the choice is difficult, the statement is ambiguous; and such in fact is the case here. The first alternative was chosen in paraphrasing §10(3) as §10(4), but the other alternative would have been just about equally reasonable.

Grouping also had to be decided in the first step of all, from §10(1) to §10(2); we had to decide whether to construe §10(1) as of the form 'if *p* then *q*', where '*p*' answers to 'J or S' and '*q*' answers to the rest, or to construe §10(1) rather as of the form '*p* unless *q*', where '*p*' answers to 'if J or S then neither A nor M and D' and '*q*'

answers to 'C and T'. In other words, we had to decide between
these two versions of §2(5): first, the 'then' clause reaches clear to
the end and the 'unless' clause qualifies only the matter from 'then'
onwards, or, second, the 'then' clause reaches only to 'unless' and the
'unless' clause governs everything from 'if' onwards. But the reader
will probably agree, on rereading §2(5), that the former choice is
more natural; the hypothesis 'if Jones is ill or Smith is away' seems
most naturally regarded as a hypothesis governing the entire re-
mainder of the sentence.

Exercises

1. Express each of the five senses of 'pretty little girls' camp'
unambiguously and yet as idiomatically as possible. (No recourse
to parentheses.)

2. Announcements of a Republican political meeting were recently posted in Cambridge, Mass., reading 'No Third Term Rally.'
By imposing various groupings, how many different senses can you
attach to this? Try to express each of these senses unambiguously
and idiomatically.

§ 12. Verbal Cues to Grouping

Within ordinary language the intended grouping has sometimes to
be guessed, as noted in § 11, and sometimes to be inferred from
unsystematic cues. One such cue was noted in the third paragraph
of § 11; and there are others.

The 'if . . . then' idiom never leaves any ambiguity of grouping
so far as the bounds of its first component are concerned; for that
component necessarily begins at 'if' and runs clear up to 'then'. The
case of 'neither . . . nor' is precisely analogous; and likewise
'either . . . or'. This may indeed explain why 'either . . . or' is so
commonly used instead of its briefer equivalent 'or.' Consider, e.g.,
the hopelessly ambiguous compound:

(1)   Jones came and Smith stayed or Robinson left.

This could be construed either as the result of joining 'Jones came
and Smith stayed' with 'Robinson left' by 'or' or as the result of join-

28

ing 'Jones came' with 'Smith stayed or Robinson left' by 'and'; and the two versions are by no means equivalent. With help of 'either', however, the first version can be indicated thus:

(2)   Either Jones came and Smith stayed or Robinson left,

and the second version thus:

(3)   Jones came and either Smith stayed or Robinson left.

Since the first component of an 'either . . . or' compound must comprise everything from 'either' to 'or' and nothing more, (2) and (3) are unambiguous. 'Both' serves similarly in support of 'and'.

A cue to grouping is sometimes achieved also by introducing the vacuous phrase 'it is the case that' and balancing it with another 'that'. Thus the ambiguity of:

(4)   Jones came or Smith stayed and Robinson left

might be resolved by the phrasing:

(5)   It is the case that Jones came or Smith stayed and that Robinson left.

Reasoning that the two occurrences of 'that' in (5) are surely coordinate, and noting further that the second 'that' clause is necessarily a second component of the 'and' compound, we conclude that the first 'that' clause is the other component of the 'and' compound and hence that it runs all the way to 'and'. We are thus led to construe the whole as the conjunction of 'Jones came or Smith stayed' with 'Robinson left'. The intended grouping in (5) might be rendered yet more emphatic and obvious by inserting 'both' after 'case'.

Sometimes the phrase 'it is not the case that', as a substitute for 'not', provides a cue to grouping by virtue simply of its ponderousness. Thus the compound:

> Jones came but it is not the case that Smith stayed and Robinson left

is obviously to be construed as the 'but' compound, or conjunction, whose first component is 'Jones came' and whose second component is the denial of 'Smith stayed and Robinson left'. The wordiness of the expression 'it is not the case that' suggests that this expression is intended to govern the long clause 'Smith stayed and Robinson left' rather than just the short clause 'Smith stayed'. If the speaker had wanted only to deny 'Smith stayed' he would have said 'Smith did not stay' rather than 'it is not the case that Smith stayed'.

Insertion of other seemingly idle particles can accomplish this same effect of suggesting grouping through ponderousness. Examples are the insertion of 'furthermore' or 'also' after 'and,' and the insertion of 'else' after 'or'. The version of the ambiguous compound (4) which (5) expresses could have been expressed fairly successfully thus:

(6)   Jones came or Smith stayed and furthermore Robinson left;

and the other version of (4) could be expressed thus:

(7)   Jones came or else Smith stayed and Robinson left.

Because the connectives 'and furthermore' and 'or else' suggest greater breaks than 'or' and 'and', we tend to interpret (6) as an 'and' compound whose first component is an 'or' compound, and to interpret (7) as an 'or' compound whose second component is an 'and' compound.

Exercise

Indicate which of the two translations:

(i)   ~(~(Rutgers will get the pennant . Hobart will be runner-up) . ~ Rzymski will be disqualified),

(ii)   Rutgers will get the pennant . ~(~ Hobart will be runner-up . ~ Rzymski will be disqualified)

conforms in your opinion to the most likely meaning of the words:

(iii)   Rutgers will get the pennant and Hobart will be runner-up unless Rzymski is disqualified.

Or is (iii) flatly ambiguous? What would you suggest by way of unambiguous idiomatic renderings respectively of (i) and (ii)?

§ 13. Paraphrasing Inward

The task of translating an elaborate compound such as §2(5) into terms of conjunction and denial consists in part, we have seen, in discerning the intended groupings. But when we have decided on one or another grouping, by dint of verbal cues or guesswork, we must thereafter take care to preserve it in the final translation. Preparatory to passing from §10(1) to §10(2), for example, we decided to construe the segment:

(1)   neither A nor M and D unless C and T

of §10(1) as a single unit corresponding to the 'q' of 'if p then q.' Accordingly, applying the rule whereby 'if p then q' goes into '$\sim(p . \sim q)$', we translated §10(1) into the form §10(2), wherein the denial sign '$\sim$' comes to be applied to (1). It is important thereafter to remember that this denial sign applies to (1) as a whole, just as the denial sign of '$\sim q$' (in '$\sim(p . \sim q)$') applies to 'q' as a whole. Obviously we should be in error if in subsequent steps we were to handle the segment:

(2) $\sim$ neither A nor M and D unless C and T

of §10(2) as if it were built from '$\sim$ neither A nor M and D' and 'C and T' by 'unless', instead of being built from (1) as a whole by '$\sim$'.

A similar precaution is necessary after passing from §10(3) to §10(4). This transition involves construing (1) above as of the form 'p unless q', where 'q' answers to 'C and T'. The rule whereby 'p unless q' goes into '$\sim(\sim p . \sim q)$' causes 'C and T' as a whole to fall under a denial sign, corresponding to the denial sign of '$\sim q$' in '$\sim(\sim p . \sim q)$'. Thus we should be in error if in subsequent steps we were to handle the segment '$\sim$ C and T' of §10(4) as if it were the conjunction of '$\sim$C' and 'T', rather than the denial of 'C and T'.

Confusions of this kind can be avoided by adhering to this simple canon: *First paraphrase the main connective of the whole compound; then paraphrase the main connective of a continuous segment of verbal text which is marked off by logical signs; and continue thus as long as verbal expressions of statement composition remain.* By 'logical signs' here are meant just '$\sim$', '.', '(', and ')'; and a continuous segment of verbal text (containing no logical signs) is said to be *marked off* by logical signs if it abuts on logical signs at both sides, or if one side abuts on a logical sign and the other side begins or ends the whole context.

Thus we begin, in the example of § 10, by picking out the main connective of §10(1)—viz. 'if . . . then'. We construe §10(1) in its entirety as having the form 'if p then q'. Then we translate it into §10(2) according to the rule for translating 'if p then q' into conjunction and denial. Next we pick a continuous verbal segment of §10(2) which is bounded by logical signs, and paraphrase its main connective; in fact we pick 'J or S', which is bounded in §10(2) by the logical signs '(' and '.'. This step leads us to §10(3). As a third step we pick a continuous verbal segment of §10(3), viz. (1), which is bounded in §10(3) by logical signs (viz. '~' and ')'); and we paraphrase its main connective, thus passing to §10(4). We continue in this wise to §10(5) and finally to §10(6). The order of the second and third steps here could just as well have been reversed, so far as our canon is concerned. But the canon does prevent us, for example, from translating the verbal segment 'neither A nor M and D' ahead of the longer segment (1); this shorter segment does not appear marked off by logical signs until we reach the stage §10(4), and it only then becomes ripe for translation. Thus in particular the fallacy of construing (2) as an 'unless' compound of '~ neither A nor M and D' and 'C and T' is automatically ruled out. Our canon requires us to translate the verbal segment (1) of §10(2) as a whole; and the initial '~' of (2), as an inert fragment of the context, plays no role in the internal translation of (1).

The fallacy of handling the '~ C and T' of §10(4) as a conjunction of '~C' and 'T' is automatically excluded in similar fashion. Our canon requires that we translate the *verbal* segment 'C and T,' and not the half verbal and half symbolic segment '~ C and T'; the initial '~' of '~ C and T' remains an inert fragment of the context, as did the '~' of (2).

Thus, in general, our canon provides automatically that any continuous verbal segment marked off by logical signs be handled as a single unit; the segment 'C and T' of §10(4) comes automatically to be handled as a single unit governed by '~', and similarly for the segment (1) of §10(2).

But the following supplementary canon, exemplified in the last steps of § 10, is also important: *on paraphrasing a verbal segment into a symbolic conjunction, enclose the whole in parentheses in case it occurs immediately after* '~'. If in paraphrasing the 'C and T' of §10(5) as 'C . T' we had failed to enclose the latter in parentheses, the protection noted in the preceding paragraph would have gone for naught; for '~C . T' is precisely the version of '~ C and T' which we wanted to avoid. The case is similar with the 'M and D' of §10(5), and also with the 'neither A nor M and D' of §10(4); the one goes into '(M . D)' and the other into '(~A . ~ M and D)', outside parentheses being needed in each case in view of the antecedent '~'.

Exercises

1. Which of the following become indistinguishable on translation into terms of conjunction and denial?

> If this lake does not drain northward, then we are in the basin of the Amazon but not in Brazil.

> This lake drains northward or else we are in the basin of the Amazon but not in Brazil.

> It is not the case both that this lake does not drain northward and that if we are in the basin of the Amazon we are in Brazil.

2. Translate the following into terms of conjunction and denial:

> Jones will sell his car and mortgage his home unless the new mail-order campaign breaks the Dripsweet monopoly and restores freedom of competition.

> If the hill people prove recalcitrant and the colonists complain of further incursions, then the boundary will be moved to Thorpeport; but the port itself will remain under the control of the Junta unless a remanding order is forthcoming from the Colonial Office.

II • TRUTH-FUNCTIONAL
TRANSFORMATIONS

§ 14. Substitution in Truth-Functional Schemata

FROM AMONG the various logical locutions (§1), only certain ones
have concerned us thus far, viz. statement connectives, and more
especially the truth-functional ones. The pattern according to which
the components of a compound statement are knit together by such
connectives may be called, in a loose phrase, the *truth-functional
structure* of the compound. Truth-functional structure is thus a part
of logical structure (§1). Now just as those statements have been
called logically true which are true by virtue solely of their logical
structure (§1), so those may be called *truth-functionally true* which
are true by virtue solely of their truth-functional structure. Thus
truth-functional truth is a special case of logical truth. We may
speak likewise of truth-functional equivalence and implication, as
special cases of logical equivalence and implication.[1] These notions
have yet to be sharpened, and associated techniques have to be developed. Techniques are wanted, for example, for transforming
compound statements into others, differently compounded, to which
they are truth-functionally equivalent; insofar as the new compounds
are simpler or clearer than the old, such techniques are of obvious
practical utility.

Treatment of truth-functional structure is facilitated by using
the letters 'p', 'q', etc. in place of statements, e.g. in the fashion 'if
p then q' or '$\sim(p \cdot \sim q)$'—as has indeed already been done in
§§10–13. This device serves to set forth the structure of a compound
in abstraction from any specific meanings of the components, since

---

[1] In *Mathematical Logic* truth-functional truth is called tautology, and
truth-functional equivalence and implication are called tautologous
equivalence and implication.

the letters have no meaning in themselves. Thus '$\sim(p \cdot \sim q)$' portrays the common truth-functional structure of the two compounds:

$\sim$(all three fixtures are original . $\sim$ the chest is valuable),

$\sim$(no warning was posted . $\sim$ the proprietor is liable).

The one compound is got from '$\sim(p \cdot \sim q)$' by substitution of 'all three fixtures are original' for 'p' and 'the chest is valuable' for 'q'; while the other compound is got from '$\sim(p \cdot \sim q)$' by different substitution.

The letters 'p', 'q', 'r', and 's', also with subscripts in the fashion 'p_1', 'p_2', 'q_1', 'q_n', will be called *statement letters;* and these, together with all expressions thence constructible by conjunction and denial, will be called *truth-functional schemata.* Thus the truth-functional schemata include the expressions 'p', 'q', '$\sim p$', '$\sim\sim p$', '$p \cdot q$', '$p \cdot p$', '$\sim p \cdot q$', '$p \cdot \sim q \cdot r$', '$\sim(p \cdot \sim q)$', '$\sim(\sim(p \cdot q) \cdot r)$'. No meaning is to be attached to such expressions: they serve only in the manner of diagrams, in connection with general discussions of truth-functional structure.

The notion of substitution alluded to above receives its sharp formulation with help of an auxiliary notion of *introduction.* Introduction of a statement or truth-functional schema S at a given occurrence of a statement letter L, within any schema, consists simply in putting S in place of that occurrence of L, but first enclosing S in parentheses in case S is a conjunction and L is immediately preceded by '$\sim$'. Thus introduction of the schema '$\sim(p \cdot \sim q)$' at the second occurrence of 'q' in '$q \cdot \sim(\sim r \cdot q)$' yields:

$$q \cdot \sim(\sim r \cdot \sim(p \cdot \sim q));$$

and introduction of '$p \cdot \sim q$' at the second occurrence of 'q' in '$q \cdot \sim(\sim r \cdot q)$' yields the same result. Introduction of the statement 'Jones is ill' at the occurrence of 'p' in '$\sim p$' yields '$\sim$ Jones is ill'. Introduction of:

(1)   Jones is ill . Smith is away

at the occurrence of 'p' in '$\sim p$' yields:

(2) $\sim$(Jones is ill . Smith is away).

Introduction of 'Jones is ill' at the occurrence of 'q' in '$\sim(p \cdot \sim q)$' yields:

(3) $\sim(p \cdot \sim$ Jones is ill),

which, as it happens, is neither a statement nor a truth-functional schema. Introduction of a statement may yield either a statement or a hybrid expression such as (3).

Substitution of statements or schemata for letters, in a given schema *S*, consists in introducing the statements or schemata at occurrences of the letters according to these rules: (a) *whatever is introduced at one occurrence of a letter is introduced also at all other occurrences of that letter throughout S*, and (b) *the final result is a statement or truth-functional schema.*

Thus substitution of 'Jones is ill' for '*p*' and 'Smith is away' for '*q*' in the schema '*p* . ~(*p* . *q*)' yields the statement:

(4)   Jones is ill . ~(Jones is ill . Smith is away).

Substitution of 'Jones is ill' for '*p*' and (2) for '*q*' in '*p* . *q*' likewise yields (4); and so does substitution of 'Jones is ill' for '*p*' and (1) for '*q*' in '*p* . ~*q*'. Again substitution of 'Jones is ill' for '*p*', 'Jones is ill' for '*q*', and 'Smith is away' for '*r*' in '*p* . ~(*q* . *r*)' also yields (4); there is no rule against substituting the same statement 'Jones is ill' thus for different letters '*p*' and '*q*'. On the other hand (4) cannot be got by substitution in '*p* . ~(*p* . *p*)'; introduction of 'Jones is ill' at two occurrences of '*p*' and 'Smith is away' at a third occurrence of '*p*' does not come under the head of substitution, in view of (a). Again the statement:

Jones is ill . ~ Jones is ill . Smith is away

cannot be got by substitution in '*p* . ~*q*'; replacement of '*q*' thus by (1) without adding parentheses is not introduction.

Substitution of schemata is analogous to that of statements. Substitution of the schema '*p* . *q*' for '*p*' and the schema '*r*' for '*q*' in '*p* . ~(*p* . *q*)', e.g., yields the schema:

(5) $p . q . \sim(p . q . r).$

Substitution of schemata for letters turns schemata into schemata and substitution of statements for letters turns schemata into statements.

Joint substitution of statements or schemata for letters, in two or more given schemata, consists in introducing the statements or schemata at occurrences of the letters in all those given schemata according to the following rules: (a′) *whatever is introduced at one occurrence of a letter is introduced also at all other occurrences of that letter throughout all the given schemata,* and (b′) *the final results are statements or truth-functional schemata.* Thus the statements (4) and:

(6)   ∼(Jones is ill . Smith is away . ∼ Robinson is here)

proceed from the respective schemata:

(7) $p \cdot \sim(p \cdot q)$, $\sim(p \cdot q \cdot \sim r)$

by joint substitution of 'Jones is ill' for 'p', 'Smith is away' for 'q', and 'Robinson is here' for 'r'. Again the schemata (5) and:

(8) $\sim(p \cdot q \cdot r \cdot \sim p)$

proceed from the respective schemata (7) by joint substitution of '$p \cdot q$' for 'p', 'r' for 'q', and 'p' for 'r'.

Expressions may be obtainable respectively from two schemata by substitution, and not yet by joint substitution. E.g., (4) can be got by substitution in '$p \cdot \sim(p \cdot q)$', and (6) can be got by substitution in '$\sim(r \cdot q \cdot \sim p)$', but (4) and (6) cannot be got by joint substitution in '$p \cdot \sim(p \cdot q)$' and '$\sim(r \cdot q \cdot \sim p)$'.

Exercises

1. Which of the schemata:

(i) $\sim(p \cdot q \cdot \sim(p \cdot q \cdot r \cdot s) \cdot \sim r \cdot s)$,

(ii) $\sim(\sim p \cdot \sim(\sim p \cdot \sim p) \cdot \sim p)$,

(iii) $\sim(\sim(p \cdot q) \cdot \sim\sim(p \cdot q) \cdot \sim(p \cdot q))$,

(iv) $\sim(\sim q \cdot \sim(\sim q \cdot \sim q \cdot q) \cdot \sim q)$,

(v) $\sim(\sim(q \cdot \sim r) \cdot \sim(\sim(q \cdot \sim r) \cdot \sim q \cdot r) \cdot \sim(q \cdot \sim r))$

can be got by substitution in '$\sim(p \cdot \sim(p \cdot q) \cdot \sim r)$'? Explain.

2. If in the above exercise your answer with regard to (i) was affirmative, then present a new schema such that (i) and this new schema can be got by joint substitution respectively in:

(vi) $\sim(p \cdot \sim(p \cdot q) \cdot \sim r)$, $\sim(r \cdot \sim(p \cdot s \cdot r))$.

Correspondingly for (ii), (iii), (iv), (v).

§ 15. Instances

A statement which can be got from a schema by substitution (§14) will be called an *instance* of that schema. Thus §14(4) is an instance of each of the schemata 'p . $\sim(p$. $q)$', 'p . q', 'p . $\sim q$', and 'p . $\sim(q$. $r)$'. Also, trivially, §14(4) is an instance of the schema 'p'; any statement is an instance of any letter. On the other hand §14(5) is not an instance of 'p . $\sim(p$. $q)$', nor of anything else; for it is not a statement.

When one schema is formed from another by substitution, e.g., 'p . $\sim(p$. $q)$' from 'q . $\sim r$', all statements which are instances of the new schema are instances also of the original one. This becomes obvious on considering any random case—say §14(4); this is obtainable as an instance of 'p . $\sim(p$. $q)$' by substituting 'Jones is ill' for 'p' and 'Smith is away' for 'q', and it is obtainable as an instance of 'q . $\sim r$' by substituting 'Jones is ill' for 'q' and 'Jones is ill . Smith is away' for 'r'. Note, on the other hand, that not all instances of 'q . $\sim r$' are instances of 'p . $\sim(p$. $q)$'; e.g. the statement:

Jones is ill . $\sim$ Smith is away

is an instance of 'q . $\sim r$' and not of 'p . $\sim(p$. $q)$'.

Several statements which can be got from as many schemata by joint substitution (§14) will be called *corresponding instances* of the respective schemata. Thus §14(4) and §14(6) are corresponding instances of the respective schemata §14 (7). If two schemata happen to have no letters in common, obviously any substitutions in the respective schemata will constitute a joint substitution; so that in such a case any instances of the respective schemata will be corresponding instances. Any instances of 'p . $\sim q$' and '$\sim r$', for example, are corresponding instances thereof; and indeed any two statements whatever are corresponding instances of any two letters.

If from two schemata we form two new ones by joint substitution, then any corresponding instances of the new schemata will be corresponding instances likewise of the original schemata. This again is a principle which becomes obvious on considering any random example. The schemata §14(7) result from joint substitution of 'r' for 'p', 'p' for 'q', and 'p . q' for 'r' in the respective schemata 'q . $\sim r$' and '$\sim(r$. $\sim p)$'. Now the corresponding instances §14(4)

39

and §14(6) of the schemata §14(7) are corresponding instances of the schemata 'q . $\sim r$' and '$\sim(r$. $\sim p)$', being obtainable from those schemata by joint substitution of 'Robinson is here' for 'p', 'Jones is ill' for 'q', and 'Jones is ill . Smith is away' for 'r'.

Exercises

1. If in Exercise 1 of §14 your answer with regard to (i) was affirmative, then write a statement which is an instance of (i), and show what substitutions would deliver this statement directly from '$\sim(p$. $\sim(p$. $q)$. $\sim r)$'. Also translate your statement into ordinary language as idiomatically as possible, using 'if . . . then', 'unless', etc. Correspondingly for (ii), (iii), (iv), (v).

2. For each of the pairs of schemata which you formed in Exercise 2 of §14 by joint substitution in the schemata (vi), present a pair of corresponding instances. Also show what joint substitutions would deliver this pair of statements directly from the schemata (vi). Translate your statements into ordinary language.

3. When the statements:

> If the watchman shot the plaintiff but did not shoot him without warning him, then the plaintiff is partly to blame,

> If the plaintiff is partly to blame then the watchman, the cashier, and the plaintiff are all partly to blame

are translated into terms of conjunction and denial, do they become instances of the respective schemata (vi) in Exercise 2, §14? Do they become corresponding instances? Explain.

§ 16. Equivalent Schemata

Two schemata will be said to be *equivalent* when they have no corresponding instances with unlike truth values. E.g., the schemata:

$$(1) \qquad p \cdot q, \qquad q \cdot p$$

are equivalent; for any corresponding instances of these will merely be conjunctions of one and the same pair of statements in a different

order, and such difference of order is immaterial to the truth value
of a conjunction.

Again, the schemata:

(2) $p \cdot {\sim}p,$ $q \cdot {\sim}q$

are equivalent. For any instance of '$p \cdot {\sim}p$' will be a conjunction of
two statements one of which is the other's denial. These two statements will be opposite in truth value, and thus their conjunction will
be false. All instances of '$p \cdot {\sim}p$' are thus false; and similar reasoning shows that all instances of '$q \cdot {\sim}q$' are false. Thus all instances
of the schemata (2) agree in truth value; so the schemata are equivalent. (The notion of corresponding instances here is trivial, for any
instances of the schemata (2) are corresponding instances; cf. §15.)

Again, the schemata:

(3) $p \cdot p,$ p

are equivalent. For let us suppose 'p' replaced in both schemata by
any one statement; i.e., let us think of '$p \cdot p$' and 'p' for the moment
not as schemata but as corresponding instances of those schemata.
If 'p' is true, then '$p \cdot p$', being a conjunction with both components
true, will be true; and if 'p' is false, then '$p \cdot p$' being a conjunction
of falsehoods, will be false. In either case, therefore, '$p \cdot p$' and 'p'
will be alike in truth value.

Again, the schemata:

(4) ${\sim}{\sim}p,$ p

are equivalent. For let us think of 'p' again as any statement. If 'p'
is true, '${\sim}p$' will be false and its denial '${\sim}{\sim}p$' in turn will be true;
while if 'p' is false, then '${\sim}p$' will be true and '${\sim}{\sim}p$' false. In either
case, therefore, '${\sim}{\sim}p$' and 'p' will be alike in truth value.

Again, the schemata:

(5) $p \cdot {\sim}(q \cdot {\sim}p),$ p

are equivalent. For think of the letters here as any statements. If 'p'
is false, then '$p \cdot {\sim}(q \cdot {\sim}p)$' is false, being a conjunction of statements one of which is false. If, on the other hand, 'p' is true, then
'${\sim}p$' becomes false and hence so does the conjunction '$q \cdot {\sim}p$',
whereupon the denial '${\sim}(q \cdot {\sim}p)$' becomes true; then '$p \cdot {\sim}(q \cdot {\sim}p)$'
is a conjunction of true statements, and is thus true.

Again, the schemata:

(6) ${\sim}(p \cdot {\sim}(q \cdot r)),$ ${\sim}(p \cdot {\sim}q) \cdot {\sim}(p \cdot {\sim}r)$

41

are equivalent. For think of the letters here as any statements. The conjunctions 'p . $\sim q$', 'p . $\sim r$', and 'p . $\sim(q$. $r)$' will all be false if their component 'p' happens to be false; accordingly their respective denials '$\sim(p$. $\sim q)$', '$\sim(p$. $\sim r)$', and '$\sim(p$. $\sim(q$. $r))$' will be true, and so also will the conjunction of these first two denials, viz. '$\sim(p$. $\sim q)$. $\sim(p$. $\sim r)$'. Thus the compounds (6) agree in truth value when 'p' is false. Next suppose rather that 'p' is true. The conjunction 'p . $\sim q$' will then be true just in case its other component '$\sim q$' is true, hence just in case 'q' is false; thus 'p . $\sim q$' will be opposite in truth value to 'q', and its denial '$\sim(p$. $\sim q)$' will accordingly have the same truth value as 'q'. Similarly '$\sim(p$. $\sim r)$' will have the same truth value as 'r', and '$\sim(p$. $\sim(q$. $r))$' will have the same truth value as 'q . r'. But the conjunction '$\sim(p$. $\sim q)$. $\sim(p$. $\sim r)$' will likewise have the same truth value as 'q . r', since its parts '$\sim(p$. $\sim q)$' and '$\sim(p$. $\sim r)$' have the respective truth values of 'q' and 'r'. Thus the compounds (6) agree in truth value when 'p' is true, as well as when 'p' is false.

Schemata which are equivalent to the same schema are equivalent to each other. For, given any corresponding instances S_1 and S_2 of two schemata F_1 and F_2 which are equivalent to a third F_3, let us perform upon F_3 the same substitutions which yielded S_1 and S_2 when performed on F_1 and F_2. (If there are variables in F_3 which did not occur in F_1 and F_2, statements may be substituted for them at random.) Now the result S_3 must have the same truth value as S_1, since S_1 and S_3 are corresponding instances of equivalent schemata F_1 and F_3; and similarly S_3 must have the same truth value as S_2. Hence S_1 and S_2 have the same truth value.

From the equivalences (4) and (3), to illustrate, we can infer that '$\sim \sim p$' and 'p . p' are equivalent; and from the equivalences (4) and (5) we can infer that '$\sim \sim p$' and 'p . $\sim(q$. $\sim p)$' are equivalent.

Exercises

1. Illustrate the argument of the next to the last paragraph above, taking F_1, F_2, and F_3 from (3) and (5) and choosing appropriate statements S_1, S_2, S_3.

2. To show that two schemata are not equivalent, we have only to present a pair of corresponding instances such that one happens to be true and the other false. Show in this way that the schemata (vi) of Exercise 2, §14, are not equivalent.

§ 17. Truth-Functional Equivalence

Statements which are corresponding instances of equivalent truth-functional schemata are called *truth-functionally equivalent* (cf. §14). Thus the statements:

Jones is ill . Jones is ill,   Jones is ill

are truth-functionally equivalent, being corresponding instances of the equivalent schemata §16(3). Again the statements:

(1)   ∼(Jones is guilty . ∼(Smith is innocent . Robinson lied)),

(2)   ∼(Jones is guilty . ∼ Smith is innocent) . ∼(Jones is guilty . ∼ Robinson lied)

are truth-functionally equivalent, being corresponding instances of the equivalent schemata §16(6).

It is convenient also to apply the term 'truth-functionally equivalent' to statements which are expressed with help of ordinary verbal connectives rather than just '.' and '∼', but which go over into corresponding instances of equivalent truth-functional schemata when translated into terms of '.' and '∼' according to the principles of translation set up in Chapter I. Thus the statements:

If Jones is guilty, then Smith is innocent and Robinson lied,

If Jones is guilty then Smith is innocent, and if Jones is guilty then Robinson lied

are truth-functionally equivalent in view of the fact that they go over into (1) and (2) when translated according to §§3, 7.

Truth-functionally equivalent statements are of course alike in truth value; but statements can also be alike in truth value without being truth-functionally equivalent. The statements:

If Magog is north of Derby, it is in Canada,

Magog is north of Derby and in Canada,

or in symbols:

∼(Magog is north of Derby . ∼ Magog is in Canada),

Magog is north of Derby . Magog is in Canada,

are both true and yet not truth-functionally equivalent; they are not corresponding instances of any equivalent truth-functional schemata. They are corresponding instances of the schemata '$\sim(p \cdot \sim q)$' and '$p \cdot q$', but these schemata are not equivalent, because corresponding instances with unlike truth values can be found for them. We have only to put a falsehood for 'p' and any statement for 'q' to obtain corresponding instances of '$\sim(p \cdot \sim q)$' and '$p \cdot q$' which are respectively true and false.

Truth-functionally equivalent statements not only agree in truth value, but do so by virtue of their structure in terms of truth functions alone. They continue to agree in truth value when their constituent *simple statements*—those which are not denials or conjunctions in turn—are varied at will. Statements which are truth-functionally equivalent would commonly be described as "having the same meaning", or as "saying the same thing in different language".

Exercise

Give a statement to which:

(i)   Tufa floats, and is not volcanic in origin unless it floats

is truth-functionally equivalent according to §16(5). Give another to which the denial of (i) is equivalent according to §16(6). What substitutions for the variables of §16(5)–(6) are involved?

§ 18. Replacement

Equivalence allows an operation analogous to the familiar mathematical one of putting equals for equals. Just as in arithmetic the equation '$3 \times 4 = 12$' leads to the equation '$\sqrt{3 \times 4} = \sqrt{12}$', so in logic the equivalence of '$\sim\sim p$' and 'p' leads, e.g., to the equivalence of '$\sim(q \cdot \sim\sim p)$' and '$\sim(q \cdot p)$'.

The general principle to this effect will be proved in the present section. It may be called the *principle of replacement*. It runs as follows: *if within a given schema we replace a part by another schema which is equivalent to that part, the whole resulting schema*

44

will be equivalent to the whole original schema. But first the word
'replace' here must be submitted to certain refinements, on the score
of parentheses. We do not want to regard passage from '$\sim p \cdot p$' to
'$\sim\sim\sim p$' as a case of *replacing* '$p \cdot p$' by '$\sim\sim p$', for '$p \cdot p$' does not
occur as a component in '$\sim p \cdot p$'; the '$\sim$' in '$\sim p \cdot p$' belongs to the
first 'p', and '$\sim p$' as a whole is conjoined to the second 'p'. Conversely, also, we do not want to regard passage from '$\sim\sim\sim p$' to
'$\sim p \cdot p$' as a case of replacing '$\sim\sim p$' by '$p \cdot p$'; replacement of
'$\sim\sim p$' by '$p \cdot p$' is to be understood rather as leading from '$\sim\sim\sim p$'
to '$\sim(p \cdot p)$'. Thus, in general, when the part said to be *replaced*
is a conjunction, we are to understand that it does not occur *immediately* after a denial sign; at least a parenthesis must intervene. And
when the schema replacing a given part is a conjunction, we are to
understand that it is first to be enclosed in parentheses in case it is
to occur immediately after a denial sign. If, on the other hand, the
replaced part is a conjunction bounded by parentheses, and the
schema which replaces it is not a conjunction, replacement is to be
understood as involving removal of parentheses; thus replacement
of '$p \cdot p$' by '$\sim\sim p$' in '$\sim(p \cdot p)$' is to be understood as yielding
'$\sim\sim\sim p$', not '$\sim(\sim\sim p)$'. The latter is foreign to our notation.

Preparatory to proving the general principle of replacement, it
is convenient to prove two special cases: (i) *the denials of any two
equivalent schemata are equivalent,* and (ii) *if to each of two
equivalent schemata we conjoin some one schema, the two resulting
schemata are equivalent.*

(i) will now be proved. An example will be developed in
bracketed inserts interpolated in the abstract argument, to facilitate
understanding. We start, then, with any two equivalent schemata
[e.g. '$\sim\sim p$' and '$p \cdot p$'; cf. §16], and from these we form new
schemata ['$\sim\sim\sim p$' and '$\sim(p \cdot p)$'] by applying '$\sim$' to each of the
original schemata (and adding parentheses to either of the original
schemata if it happens to have the form of a conjunction). Now we
want to show that the new schemata are equivalent to each other;
i.e., that any corresponding instances of them will agree in truth
value (cf. §16). Consider, then, any corresponding instances of the
new schemata [e.g. '$\sim\sim\sim$ Jones is ill' and '$\sim$(Jones is ill . Jones is
ill)']. These two statements will be denials of two statements
['$\sim\sim$Jones is ill' and 'Jones is ill . Jones is ill'] which are corresponding instances of the original schemata ['$\sim\sim p$' and '$p \cdot p$']. But, since
the original schemata are equivalent, corresponding instances thereof

will agree in truth value; and accordingly their denials will also agree in truth value, being false or true according as the former are true or false.

(ii) will next be proved. We start with any two equivalent schemata [e.g. '$\sim\sim p$' and '$p \cdot p$'], and to each of these we conjoin an additional schema [e.g. '$q \cdot \sim(q \cdot r)$'] so as to form two new schemata [e.g. '$\sim\sim p \cdot q \cdot \sim(q \cdot r)$' and '$p \cdot p \cdot q \cdot \sim(q \cdot r)$', or perhaps '$q \cdot \sim(q \cdot r) \cdot \sim\sim p$' and '$q \cdot \sim(q \cdot r) \cdot p \cdot p$']. We want to show that the two new schemata thus formed are equivalent—i.e., that any corresponding instances of the new schemata will agree in truth value. Consider, then, any two corresponding instances of the two new schemata [e.g. '$\sim\sim$Jones is ill . Smith is away . $\sim$(Smith is away . Robinson is here)' and 'Jones is ill . Jones is ill . Smith is away . $\sim$(Smith is away . Robinson is here)']. Let us call these two statements S_1 and S_2. They consist respectively of corresponding instances ['$\sim\sim$Jones is ill' and 'Jones is ill . Jones is ill'] of the two original schemata, conjoined in each case with one and the same additional statement ['Smith is away . $\sim$(Smith is away . Robinson is here)']. Now if this additional statement is false, the conjunctions S_1 and S_2 will both be false and thus alike in truth value. If, on the other hand, this additional statement is true, the conjunction S_1 will be true or false according as its other part ['$\sim\sim$Jones is ill'] is true or false; and correspondingly for S_2. But that other part of S_1 and that other part of S_2 are alike in truth value, being corresponding instances of the original equivalent schemata ['$\sim\sim p$', '$p \cdot p$']; hence S_1 and S_2 are again alike in truth value.

We are now ready to prove the general principle of replacement. Suppose we are given any schema F [e.g. '$\sim(p \cdot q \cdot \sim(r \cdot \sim\sim p \cdot q) \cdot \sim p)$'], and that we replace any part of it F_0 [e.g. '$\sim\sim p$'] by an equivalent G_0 [e.g. '$p \cdot p$'], thus obtaining a new schema G ['$\sim(p \cdot q \cdot \sim(r \cdot p \cdot p \cdot q) \cdot \sim p)$']. We want to show that F and G are equivalent. Now F_0 must have occurred in F either denied or else conjoined with something. [It occurs conjoined with 'q' in the fashion '$\sim\sim p \cdot q$'.] Let us call this denial or conjunction F_1. Now F_1 in turn, if it is not the whole of F, must occur in F either denied or conjoined with something. [It occurs conjoined with 'r' in the fashion '$r \cdot \sim\sim p \cdot q$'.] Let us call this denial or conjunction F_2. Continuing in this fashion, we get a series of schemata F_0, F_1, F_2 . . . , F [viz. '$\sim\sim p$', '$\sim\sim p \cdot q$', '$r \cdot \sim\sim p \cdot q$', '$\sim(r \cdot \sim\sim p \cdot q)$', '$\sim(r \cdot \sim\sim p \cdot q) \cdot \sim p$', '$p \cdot q \cdot \sim(r \cdot \sim\sim p \cdot q) \cdot \sim p$', '$\sim(p \cdot q \cdot$

$\sim(r \cdot \sim\sim p \cdot q) \cdot \sim p)$'] such that each is either the denial of its predecessor or else a conjunction of its predecessor with something. The corresponding parts of G, together with G itself, form a similar series $G_0, G_1, G_2 \ldots , G$ [viz. '$p \cdot p$', '$p \cdot p \cdot q$', '$r \cdot p \cdot p \cdot q$', '$\sim(r \cdot p \cdot p \cdot q)$', '$\sim(r \cdot p \cdot p \cdot q) \cdot \sim p$', '$p \cdot q \cdot \sim(r \cdot p \cdot p \cdot q) \cdot \sim p$', '$\sim(p \cdot q \cdot \sim (r \cdot p \cdot p \cdot q) \cdot \sim p)$']. Now F_1 and G_1 are either the denials of F_0 and G_0 or else conjunctions of F_0 and G_0 with some one schema; by (i) or (ii), therefore, the equivalence of F_1 and G_1 follows from that of F_0 and G_0. Similarly the equivalence of F_2 and G_2 follows from that of F_1 and G_1; and so on, until we conclude with the equivalence of F and G.

Exercise

Illustrate the three proofs of this section again, using the pair §16(6) instead of '$\sim\sim p$' and '$p \cdot p$', and taking F as:

$$\sim(\sim(p \cdot q \cdot \sim\sim(p \cdot \sim(q \cdot r))) \cdot \sim r).$$

§ 19. Transformation

Forward transformation of a given schema F_1 [e.g. '$p \cdot \sim\sim(q \cdot r)$'] *by* a given pair of schemata G_1 and G_2 [e.g. §16(4)] consists of the following operations: first we make joint substitutions in G_1 and G_2 so as to obtain schemata G_1' and G_2' [e.g. '$\sim\sim(q \cdot r)$' and '$q \cdot r$'] where G_1' is part (or all) of F_1; then we replace G_1' in F_1 by G_2'. Now it is easily shown that *the result* F_2 ['$p \cdot q \cdot r$'] *is equivalent to F_1 whenever G_2 is equivalent to G_1.* By §15, any corresponding instances of G_1' and G_2' will be corresponding instances also of G_1 and G_2, and will thus agree in truth value in view of the equivalence of G_1 and G_2 (cf. §16). Hence G_1' and G_2' are equivalent; and consequently so are F_1 and F_2, by §18.

In particular, F_1 and F_2 may coincide respectively with G_1' and G_2'. Forward transformation of '$p \cdot \sim(p \cdot \sim p)$' by §16(5) yields '$p$'. Here F_1 and F_2 are:

(1) $\qquad\qquad p \cdot \sim(p \cdot \sim p), \qquad\qquad p,$

and G_1 and G_2 are §16(5), and G_1' and G_2' are simply (1) again. The pair (1) is one which issues directly from §16(5) by joint substitution. But the inference of the equivalence (1) from the equivalence §16(5) is just a special application of the general principle italicized above.

Inference according to the principle of replacement (§18) can likewise be handled as a special case of the principle italicized above. The equivalence of the schemata:

(2) $\qquad p \cdot \sim(p \cdot \sim p), \qquad\qquad p \cdot \sim(q \cdot \sim q),$

e.g., follows from the equivalence §16(2) according to §18; but we can account for the equivalence (2) equally well in terms of forward transformation of '$p \cdot \sim(p \cdot \sim p)$' into '$p \cdot \sim(q \cdot \sim q)$' by §16(2). In this case F_1 and F_2 are (2), and G_1 and G_2 are §16(2), and G_1' and G_2' are simply §16(2) over again; the joint substitution in G_1 and G_2 which is supposed to yield G_1' and G_2' can be thought of in this case as mere substitution of 'p' for 'p'—a substitution which changes nothing.

It should be noted that forward transformation of a given schema by a given pair need not give a unique result. Forward transformation of '$\sim\sim p \cdot \sim\sim q$' by §16(4) yields '$\sim\sim p \cdot q$' and also yields '$p \cdot \sim\sim q$'. Forward transformation of '$p \cdot q$' by §16(4), on the other hand, yields nothing; for there is no way of substituting in the '$\sim\sim p$' of §16(4) so as to get part (or all) of '$p \cdot q$'.

Backward transformation by a pair G_1 and G_2 is forward transformation by the reverse pair G_2 and G_1. Thus whereas forward transformation of '$p \cdot \sim\sim(q \cdot r)$' by §16(4) yields '$p \cdot q \cdot r$', backward transformation of '$p \cdot q \cdot r$' by §16(4) yields '$p \cdot \sim\sim(q \cdot r)$'. By *transformation*, more generally, will be meant forward and backward transformation indifferently; thus '$p \cdot \sim\sim(q \cdot r)$' is transformable into '$p \cdot q \cdot r$' by §16(4) and vice versa. In general, *if F_1 is transformable into F_2 by a pair of mutually equivalent schemata, then F_1 and F_2 are equivalent.* This was established above for forward transformation; and it holds equally for backward transformation, since backward transformation by a given pair of equivalents is simply forward transformation by the same equivalents taken in the opposite order.

The transformations which have been carried out in application to schemata can be carried out equally well in direct application to the statements which are instances of the schemata. Forward transformation of a statement S_1 by a pair of schemata G_1 and G_2 can be explained as consisting of these operations: first we make joint substitutions in G_1 and G_2 so as to obtain statements G_1' and G_2' where G_1' is part of S_1; then we replace G_1' in S_1 by G_2'. In short, *forward transformation of S_1 by the pair G_1 and G_2 consists in replacing an instance of G_1 within S_1 by a corresponding instance of G_2* (cf. §15). Analogously for backward transformation and for transformation generally.

Just as forward transformation of the schema '$p \cdot \sim\sim(q \cdot r)$' by §16(4) yields '$p \cdot q \cdot r$', so forward transformation of the statement:

Jones came $\cdot \sim\sim$(Smith stayed $\cdot$ Robinson left)

by §16(4) yields:

Jones came $\cdot$ Smith stayed $\cdot$ Robinson left.

Transformation of statements thus differs from that of schemata only in that statements appear in place of letters. Instead of transforming a schema F_1 into a schema F_2, we transform an instance S_1 of F_1 into a corresponding instance S_2 of F_2. Just as transformation by a pair of equivalent schemata leads from a schema F_1 to an equivalent schema F_2, so it leads from a statement S_1 to a truth-functionally equivalent statement S_2; for corresponding instances of equivalent truth-functional schemata are truth-functionally equivalent (cf. §17).

Exercises

1. How many different schemata can be obtained each through a single transformation of:

(i) $p \cdot q \cdot \sim(p \cdot q \cdot r)$

by §16(1)? What joint substitutions for the 'p' and 'q' of §16(1) are involved in each of these cases?

2. How many different schemata can be obtained each through a single backward transformation of (i) by §16(4)? Which of the results are susceptible in turn to forward transformation by §16(6)? What joint substitutions in §16(6) are involved?

§ 20. Proofs of Equivalence

If a schema is transformed successively, by one or another pair of equivalents at each step, we can conclude that the end product is equivalent to the original. E.g., since the second of the schemata §19(2) is transformable into the first of the schemata §19(2) by §16(2), and the resulting schema is transformable in turn into 'p' by §16(5), we can conclude that the schemata:

(1) $p \cdot \sim(q \cdot \sim q)$, p

are equivalent. This is merely an inference of the equivalence of the schemata (1) from the equivalence of the schemata §19(2) and the equivalence of the schemata §19(1), in conformity with the principle at the end of §16.

Proofs of equivalence by successive transformation, in the above fashion, may conveniently be recorded by simply setting down the successive stages of transformation and citing at the right the pairs of equivalents whereby the transformations are made. The argument which established the equivalence of the schemata (1), above, may be written thus:

Proof. $p \cdot \sim(p \cdot \sim p)$ §16(2)
                  p §16(5)

The entry at the right of the first line indicates that that line is got from the first of the schemata (1) through a transformation by §16(2), and the entry at the right of the second line indicates that the 'p' of the second line is got from the first line through a transformation by §16(5).

Further equivalences and proofs follow.

(2) $p \cdot q \cdot \sim q$, $r \cdot \sim r$
Proof. $p \cdot p \cdot \sim p$ §16(2)
                                  $p \cdot \sim p$ §16(3)
                                  $r \cdot \sim r$ §16(2)

(3) $\sim(p \cdot \sim(q_1 \cdot q_2 \cdot \ \ldots \ \cdot q_n))$,
                            $\sim(p \cdot \sim q_1) \cdot \sim(p \cdot \sim q_2) \cdot \ \ldots \ \cdot \sim(p \cdot \sim q_n)$

Proof (for any given n):

$\sim(p \cdot \sim q_1) \cdot \sim(p \cdot \sim(q_2 \cdot \ \ldots \ \cdot q_n))$ §16(6)
$\sim(p \cdot \sim q_1) \cdot \sim(p \cdot \sim q_2) \cdot \sim(p \cdot \sim(q_3 \cdot \ \ldots \ \cdot q_n))$ §16(6)

and so on.

50

(4) $\sim(p \cdot q) \cdot \sim(p \cdot \sim q),$ $\sim p$

Proof. $\sim(p \cdot \sim\sim q) \cdot \sim(p \cdot \sim q)$ §16(4)

$\sim(p \cdot \sim(\sim q \cdot q))$ §16(6)

$\sim(p \cdot \sim(q \cdot \sim q))$ §16(1)

$\sim p$ (1)

But it is convenient to leave transformations by §16(1) and §16(4) tacit. We quickly learn simply to overlook questions of order in conjunctions; and we learn to regard the denying of a denial as a direct matter of removing the old denial sign, instead of applying a second denial sign and cancelling. The above proof then takes on this condensed form:

Proof. $\sim(p \cdot \sim(\sim q \cdot q))$ §16(6)

$\sim p$ (1)

Two more equivalences will be proved in the same condensed style.

(5) $p \cdot \sim(p \cdot q),$ $p \cdot \sim q$

Proof. $\sim(\sim(p \cdot \sim p) \cdot \sim(p \cdot \sim q))$ §16(6)

$p \cdot \sim q$ (1)

Preparatory to the transformation indicated in the first line of this proof, there is a tacit backward transformation of '$p \cdot \sim(p \cdot q)$' into '$\sim\sim(p \cdot \sim(p \cdot q))$' by §16(4). Preparatory to the transformation indicated in the second line, there is a tacit transformation by §16(1). Moreover, the transformation by (1) noted in that line yields not '$p \cdot \sim q$' but '$\sim\sim(p \cdot \sim q)$'; so a tacit transformation by §16(4) occurs in conclusion.

(6) $\sim(p \cdot q \cdot r) \cdot \sim(p \cdot \sim r),$ $\sim(p \cdot q) \cdot \sim(p \cdot \sim r)$

Proof. $\sim(p \cdot \sim(\sim(q \cdot r) \cdot r))$ §16(6)

$\sim(p \cdot \sim(\sim q \cdot r))$ (5)

$\sim(p \cdot q) \cdot \sim(p \cdot \sim r)$ §16(6)

Preparatory to the transformation indicated in the first line of the above proof, there is a tacit backward transformation by §16(4). Preparatory to the transformation indicated in the second line, there are two tacit transformations by §16(1). After the concluding transformation by §16(6) there is a tacit forward transformation by §16(4).

Exercises

1. Expand the proofs of (5) and (6) in the style of the first proof of (4), so as to render the tacit transformations by §16(1) and §16(4) explicit.

2. What joint substitutions in §16(6) are involved in the successive steps of the proof of (3)? Analyze the several steps in the proofs of (4)–(6) in similar fashion.

3. Using the condensed style of proof explained in connection with (4), prove the equivalence of the schemata:

$$\sim(\sim(p \cdot \sim q) \cdot \sim(\sim p \cdot q)), \qquad\qquad \sim(p \cdot q) \cdot \sim(\sim p \cdot \sim q).$$

§ 21. Alternation and Duality

Special symbols are commonly added for 'or' and 'if'. For 'p or q' the notation is '$p \mathbf{v} q$'; here '$\mathbf{v}$' stands for the Latin *vel*, which means 'or' in the inclusive sense. For 'if p then q' one encounters '$p \supset q$' and '$p \rightarrow q$'. For 'p if and only if q' one encounters '$p \equiv q$', '$p \longleftrightarrow q$', and '$p \sim q$'.

Symbols are not just for brevity. In respect of brevity '$p \mathbf{v} q$' and '$p \supset q$' improve little upon 'p or q' and 'q if p'. For that matter, '$\sim p$' and '$p \cdot q$' improve little upon 'not p' and 'p and q'. Symbols do another thing: they mark the end of verbal analysis and the readiness for formal transformation or computation. When in high-school algebra we were given problems in words, e.g. about rowing up and down stream, our first job was to work the problem into equations; our second job was to solve them. Symbols are what a problem is couched in once the first of these two jobs is done.

Thus the significance of adding the symbols '$\mathbf{v}$', '$\supset$', and '$\equiv$' would be that we proposed to bring them into the very proofs and formal laws, instead of holding to '$\sim$' and '$\cdot$' as in §20. And indeed it is common practice thus to bring them in. But the cost is substantial. The more ways we allow of writing schemata, the less frequently will equivalence be recognizable on sight. And see how the laws of equivalence are multiplied by every superfluous sign. If we admit '$\mathbf{v}$' and '$\supset$', then we must notice the equivalence of '$\sim(p \cdot \sim(q \cdot r))$'

not only to '$\sim(p \cdot \sim q) \cdot \sim(p \cdot \sim r)$' but also to '$\sim p \lor q \cdot \sim p \lor r$' and to '$p \supset q \cdot p \supset r$' and to '$\sim p \lor (q \cdot r)$' and to '$p \supset (q \cdot r)$'. Such brevity as is gained by writing '$p \lor q$' for '$\sim(\sim p \cdot \sim q)$', and '$p \supset q$' for '$\sim(p \cdot \sim q)$', is thus bought dearly.

There are, despite all this, interesting technical advantages in accepting the one redundant connective '$\lor$'—that of *alternation,* as it is called. One advantage is that denial signs cease to be needed except on single letters; denials of conjunctions resolve always to alternations. For, if we adopt the form of notation '$r \lor s$' in general as short for '$\sim(\sim r \cdot \sim s)$', then we can transcribe '$\sim(p \cdot q)$', or '$\sim(\sim\sim p \cdot \sim\sim q)$', as '$\sim p \lor \sim q$'.

Such transcription, abetted here and there by substitution of '$\sim p$' for 'p' or '$\sim q$' for 'q', serves to recast the equivalences §20(1), §16(5), and §20(3)–(6) thus:

(1) $p \cdot (q \lor \sim q),$ $p.$

(2) $p \cdot (p \lor q),$ $p.$

(3) $p \lor (q_1 \cdot q_2 \cdot \ \ldots \ \cdot q_n),$ $(p \lor q_1) \cdot (p \lor q_2) \cdot$
$\ldots \cdot (p \lor q_n).$

(4) $(p \lor q) \cdot (p \lor \sim q),$ $p.$

(5) $p \cdot (\sim p \lor q),$ $p \cdot q.$

(6) $(p \lor q \lor \sim r) \cdot (p \lor r),$ $(p \lor q) \cdot (p \lor r).$

But note the increased use of parentheses. Hitherto (§4) we had recognized parentheses only after denial signs; now we adopt them also to enclose components of conjunction and alternation. Conventions to be adopted in the next section will largely weed them out again.

One advantage conferred by '$\lor$' was, we saw, the resolving of denials of conjunctions. Another and deeper advantage is found in a *duality,* so-called, that emerges between conjunction and alternation.

In developing this point we may conveniently think of conjunction for the moment as applying to statements only pairwise; '$p \cdot q \cdot r$' can be pictured as '$(p \cdot q) \cdot r$', and '$p \cdot q \cdot r \cdot s$' as '$((p \cdot q) \cdot r) \cdot s$', and so on (cf. §3). Similarly for alternation. Conjunction, then, is fully describable by this truth condition: a conjunction of two statements is true if and only if both statements are true. But alternation is fully describable by this quite parallel falsity condition: an alternation of two statements is false if and only if both statements are false. The theory of conjunction is to truth as the theory of alternation is to falsity.

To see the force of this, consider any schema built of statement letters by conjunction or alternation or both, however complexly. Consider, further, the schema's *truth table*. It lists all the 2^n ways of assigning 'T' (for truth) and '⊥' (for falsity) to the n letters of the schema, and each of these 2^n rows it marks 'T' or '⊥' according as the whole schema comes out true or false when its letters are given the truth values shown in that row. Now what would be the effect of reinterpreting 'T' throughout the table as falsity and '⊥' as truth? Simply the effect of reinterpreting '.' throughout the schema as alternation and 'v' as conjunction.

What has been said still holds when we let our schema include denial along with conjunction and alternation. For the role of denial in a truth table is unaffected by switching the readings of 'T' and '⊥', denials of truths being false and denials of falsehoods true.

Schemata are called *duals* of each other if the truth table of the one goes over into that of the other by switching 'T' with '⊥' throughout. What we have seen, then, is that *schemata are duals if the one goes into the other by switching* '.' *with* 'v' *throughout*.

Consider, next, what happens with duals of equivalent schemata. We know from §16 that corresponding instances of equivalent schemata are both true or both false. Switching 'T' and '⊥', then, we infer that corresponding instances of the duals are both false or both true. In short, *duals of equivalent schemata are equivalent*. This circumstance enables us, with every equivalence, to get another equivalence gratis by switching '.' and 'v' to form the duals. From §16(1), §20(2), and (1) and (3)–(5) above we may thus infer without further ado the following equivalences:

(7)　　　$p \vee q$,　　　　　　　　　$q \vee p$.

(8)　　　$p \vee q \vee {\sim}q$,　　　　　　$r \vee {\sim}r$.

(9)　　　$p \vee (q \cdot {\sim}q)$,　　　　　p.

(10)　　$p \cdot (q_1 \vee q_2 \vee \ \ldots \ \vee q_n)$,　　　$(p \cdot q_1) \vee (p \cdot q_2) \vee$
　　　　　　　　　　　　　　　　　　　　$\ldots \ \vee (p \cdot q_n)$.

(11)　　$(p \cdot q) \vee (p \cdot {\sim}q)$,　　　p.

(12)　　$p \vee ({\sim}p \cdot q)$,　　　　$p \vee q$.

Also there was justified in §3 the unwritten equivalence:

　　　　　$(p \cdot q) \cdot r$,　　　　$p \cdot (q \cdot r)$,

whence we now have by duality the equivalence:

$$(p \lor q) \lor r, \qquad\qquad p \lor (q \lor r).$$

So we need no longer read an arbitrary leftward grouping into the iteration '$p \lor q \lor {\sim}r$' in (6) or those in (8) and (10).

Also we should record these mutually dual equivalences, known as *De Morgan's laws:*

(13) ${\sim}(p_1 \cdot p_2 \cdot \;\ldots\; \cdot p_n), \qquad {\sim}p_1 \lor {\sim}p_2 \lor \;\ldots\; \lor {\sim}p_n.$

(14) ${\sim}(p_1 \lor p_2 \lor \;\ldots\; \lor p_n), \qquad {\sim}p_1 \cdot {\sim}p_2 \cdot \;\ldots\; \cdot {\sim}p_n.$

These come simply of our definition of '$r \lor s$' as '${\sim}({\sim}r \cdot {\sim}s)$', with cancellation of '${\sim}{\sim}$' as it arises.

It is evident from the duality considerations themselves that we could have justified (7)–(12) without duality considerations. We could have got them by repeating the reasoning that led to their correspondents §16(1), §20(2), (1), and (3)–(5), just switching 'true' systematically with 'false' and '.' with '∨'. The benefit of recognizing duality is that we skip this duality of effort.

Exercises

1. Express '$p \equiv q$' in several relatively neat and interestingly unlike ways using conjunction, alternation, and denial.

2. Is '$p \equiv q$' dual to its own denial? Justify your answer.

3. Is the schema:

$$(p \lor q) \cdot (q \lor r) \cdot (p \lor r)$$

dual to itself? Justify your answer.

4. What equivalences may we infer by duality from §16(2)–(3)? from (2) above? from (6)?

§ 22. Normal Schemata

The truth-functional schemata were described in §14 as comprising the statement letters and all compounds thence constructible by conjunction and denial. We are now of course to understand the description as widened to include alternation.

A remarked advantage of including alternation was that we were enabled to confine denial to single letters. Denial of conjunctions can be resolved by transformation by §21(13), and denial of alternations can be resolved by transformation by §21(14).

We can do more: we can confine conjunction to letters and their denials. For, whenever an alternation stands as component of a conjunction, we can make a transformation by §21(10). This equivalence, called a *distributive law*, expresses the distributivity of conjunction into alternation. It is analogous to the familiar algebraic law of "multiplying out,"

$$x(y_1 + y_2 + \ldots + y_n) = xy_1 + xy_2 + \ldots + xy_n,$$

which expresses the distributivity of multiplication into addition.

Let us speak of statement letters and their denials collectively as *literals*. Now a schema is called an *alternational normal schema* if it is a literal or a conjunction of literals or an alternation of schemata each of which is a literal or a conjunction of literals. Negatively described, an alternational normal schema is one in which all denials are of letters and all conjunctions are of literals. So the force of the transformations just enumerated, transformations by §21(10) and §21(13)–(14), is that they suffice to turn any truth-functional schema into an alternational normal one. I am assuming tacit use of §16(4) to cancel '$\sim\sim$' and of §16(1) to permute conjunction. Thus take the schema:

(1) $\sim(\sim(p \cdot \sim(q \cdot \sim r) \cdot q) \cdot s) \cdot p.$

Successive transformations by §21(13) turn it into:

$$((p \cdot \sim(q \cdot \sim r) \cdot q) \vee \sim s) \cdot p,$$

(2) $((p \cdot (\sim q \vee r) \cdot q) \vee \sim s) \cdot p$

(with tacit cancellation of '$\sim\sim$'). Transformations by §21(10)—distributions—turn this result successively into:

$$(p \cdot (\sim q \vee r) \cdot q \cdot p) \vee (\sim s \cdot p),$$

$$(((p \cdot \sim q) \vee (p \cdot r)) \cdot q \cdot p) \vee (\sim s \cdot p),$$

(3) $(p \cdot \sim q \cdot q \cdot p) \vee (p \cdot r \cdot q \cdot p) \vee (\sim s \cdot p),$

which is an alternational normal schema. Two of the last three transformations turned on a switched version of §21(10), but the switch was just a matter of tacit §16(1).

The notations '$\sim p$' and '$p \cdot q$' are not the only notations for denial and conjunction that are current in the literature of logic. For denial some authors use '$\bar{p}$', some 'p'', some '$\neg p$'. For conjunction some use 'pq', some 'p & q', some '$p \wedge q$'. With the ascendancy of alternational normal schemata it is indeed convenient to turn to two of these variant notations part of the time: to the bar as in '$\bar{p}$' whenever only a single letter is denied, and to juxtaposition as in 'pq' whenever only literals are conjoined. Thus (3) becomes:

(3) $p\bar{q}qp \vee prqp \vee \bar{s}p$.

We observed in §21 a mechanical way of getting the dual of a schema: switch '.' with 'v'. Note that the condensed notation just adopted complicates that rule. One should think in terms still of the old notation when forming duals.

An alternational normal schema can often be reduced to a simpler alternational normal schema. Thus we can further transform (3) successively as follows:

$$r\bar{r} \vee prqp \vee \bar{s}p \qquad\qquad \text{§20(2)}$$

$$prqp \vee \bar{s}p \qquad\qquad \text{§21(9)}$$

(4) $prq \vee \bar{s}p$ §16(3)

The beauty of alternational normal schemata is not just that they lose all parentheses (under our new variant notation) and become compact. Mainly it is that they so visibly flaunt their truth conditions. Each component of the alternation registers one assortment of truth values that will make the whole true. Thus (4) will come out true if we declare 'p', 'r', and 'q' all true; also if we declare 's' false and 'p' true; and not otherwise.

Reduction to alternational normal schemata hinged on transformation by §21(10), which was like multiplying out. Now in algebra there is, over against multiplying out, no such thing as adding out; we do not have $x + yz = (x + y)(x + z)$. Multiplication is distributive through addition, but addition is not distributive through multiplication. In logic, on the other hand, duality prevails. Conjunction being distributive through alternation, alternation is perforce distributive through conjunction; see §21(3). Indeed the law of reducibility to alternational normal schemata immediately assures, by duality, a law of reducibility to what are called *conjunctional normal schemata*. These, the duals of alternational normal schemata, comprise the literals and the alternations of literals and

57

the conjunctions of schemata each of which is a literal or an alternation of literals.

Thus take (1) again. We transform it into (2) as before, but then we transform (2) by §21(3) into the conjunctional normal schema:

$$(p \vee \bar{s}) . (\bar{q} \vee r \vee \bar{s}) . (q \vee \bar{s}) . p.$$

One more notational convention is now worth while: let us understand '.' always as heavier punctuation than 'v', and so rid the conjunctional normal schemata of their parentheses. The above becomes:

$$p \vee \bar{s} . \bar{q} \vee r \vee \bar{s} . q \vee \bar{s} . p.$$

Again simplifications are possible. The above schema lends itself to these further transformations:

$$\bar{q} \vee r \vee \bar{s} . q \vee \bar{s} . p \qquad\qquad §21(2)$$

(5) $$\qquad\qquad \bar{s} \vee r . \bar{s} \vee q . p \qquad\qquad §21(6)$$

This last step depended on seeing '$\bar{q} \vee r \vee \bar{s}$' and '$q \vee \bar{s}$' as '$\bar{s} \vee r \vee \bar{q}$' and '$\bar{s} \vee q$', thus making tacit use of §21(7)—a good convention, since §21(7) is dual to the regularly tacit §16(1).

In (4) and (5), then, we have reached two concise and dissimilar equivalents of (1), one an alternational normal schema and the other a conjunctional normal schema.

Alternational ones are manifestly superior in respect of visibility of truth conditions. But the conjunctional ones have a special virtue too, as we shall see in §23.

Exercises

1. Transform (5) into alternational normal form by the usual steps, and see if it simplifies naturally to (4).

2. Transform '$pq \vee qr \vee pr$' into conjunctional normal form.

3. Express '$p \equiv (q \equiv r)$' (cf. Exercise 1 of §21) in both conjunctional and alternational normal form.

4. Translate the following into terms of conjunction and denial, using abbreviations:

Neither will the deal be closed nor will Smith keep his job unless the sales manager is called back from his vacation and the deal is closed.

Put the result into alternational normal form. Given that it is true, what possibilities remain open as regards the respective truth values of 'The deal will be closed', 'Smith will keep his job', and 'The sales manager will be called back from his vacation'?

§ 23. Validity

A schema will be called *valid* when all its instances are true. E.g., the schema '$\sim(p\bar{p})$' or 'p v $\bar{p}$' is valid, as is apparent from our earlier reflections on §16(2). A valid schema is one whose truth table (§21) marks every row 'T'.

A schema is valid if it is derived by substitution in a valid schema; for all instances of the derived schema are instances of the original (cf. §15), and hence all instances of the derived schema are true if all those of the original schema are true.

One of two equivalent schemata is valid if and only if the other is; for equivalence is agreement in truth value on the part of corresponding instances (cf. §16). E.g., since 'p v $\bar{p}$' is valid, we may infer by backward transformation by §21(8) that 'p v $\bar{p}$ v $\bar{q}$' is valid.

An alternation of literals is valid if and only if one of the literals denies another. If one literal denies another, we have the valid schema 'p v $\bar{p}$' or 'p v $\bar{p}$ v q' or the like. If no literal denies any other, we can get a false instance by putting truths for the denied letters and falsehoods for the undenied ones.

A conjunction of two or more schemata is valid if and only if each of those component schemata is valid. This is seen as follows. Since each instance of the conjunctive schema is a conjunction of instances of the component schemata, all instances of the conjunctive schema will be true if all instances of the component schemata are true; and conversely, if any of the component schemata has a false instance, each corresponding instance of the conjunctive schema will likewise be false—being a conjunction of statements not all of which are true.

Any conjunctional normal schema can accordingly be checked for validity at a glance. For a conjunctional normal schema is either (a) a literal or (b) an alteration of literals or (c) a conjunction of schemata each of which is a literal or an alternation of literals. In case (a) it is not valid; for any falsehood is an instance of any literal.

In case (b) we check for validity by seeing if one literal denies another. In case (c) we observe whether each component of the conjunction is an alternation in which one literal denies another.

In a word, *a conjunctional normal schema is valid if and only if it either is an alternation in which one literal denies another, or else is a conjunction of such alternations.*

Here, then, is a convenient test of validity of any truth-functional schema: transform it into a conjunctional normal schema by the routine of §22 and appraise the result by the above criterion.

Thus take '*pq* ∨ *pq̄* ∨ *p̄*'. We may transform it into a conjunctional normal schema thus:

$$p\bar{q} \vee \bar{p} \vee p \cdot p\bar{q} \vee \bar{p} \vee q \qquad \S21(3)$$

$$\bar{p} \vee p \vee p \cdot \bar{p} \vee p \vee \bar{q} \cdot \bar{p} \vee q \vee p \cdot \bar{p} \vee q \vee \bar{q} \qquad \S21(3)$$

This meets the validity criterion.

Actually the expansion of '*pq̄* ∨ *p̄* ∨ *p*' in the last step was idle, since '*pq̄* ∨ *p̄* ∨ *p*' is visibly valid already by virtue of its '*p̄* ∨ *p*'. As for the other half, '*pq̄* ∨ *p̄* ∨ *q*', it might better have been simplified to '*q* ∨ *p* ∨ *p̄*' by transformation by §21(12). Or, best of all, we might have begun by simplifying the original schema '*pq* ∨ *pq̄* ∨ *p̄*'; it goes directly to '*p* ∨ *p̄*' by §21(11). Early simplification is always good policy.

Exercises

1. If a conjunctional normal schema is valid and can be no further simplified by §21(1) or §21(8), how long can it be? Why no longer?

2. Test these schemata for validity:

$$\sim(p\bar{q}) \vee \sim(\bar{p}q), \qquad pq \vee \bar{p}r \vee \sim(qr), \qquad p \equiv (q \equiv (p \equiv q)).$$

§ 24. Truth-Functional Truth

Statements which are instances of valid truth-functional schemata are said to be *truth-functionally true* (cf. §14). The statement:

(1)   ∼(Jones is ill . ∼ Jones is ill),

e.g., is truth-functionally true, being an instance of the valid schema '$\sim(p\bar{p})$'. It is convenient also, on the analogy of §17, to apply the term 'truth-functionally true' to statements which are expressed with help of ordinary verbal connectives but which go over into instances of valid truth-functional schemata when translated into terms of '.', 'v', and '$\sim$'. Thus the statements:

> It is not the case that Jones is ill and not ill,
>
> If Jones is ill then Jones is ill

are truth-functionally true in view of the fact that they give way to the instance (1) of '$\sim(p\bar{p})$' when translated according to §§ 3, 4, 7. Again the statements:

> Jones is ill or Jones is not ill,
> Jones is ill unless Jones is not ill

are truth-functionally true in view of the fact that they give way to the instance:

$$\sim(\sim \text{Jones is ill} \,.\, \sim\sim \text{Jones is ill})$$

of '$\sim(p\bar{p})$' when translated according to §§ 5–6.

A truth-functionally true statement is one which is true by virtue merely of its structure in terms of truth functions. It remains true when its constituent simple statements are varied at will. The compound (1), e.g., remains true when any statement whatever is put for the two occurrences of the simple statement 'Jones is ill'; for all such variants of (1) are instances equally of the valid schema '$\sim(p\bar{p})$'.

In order to find out whether or not a given statement S is truth-functionally true it is not enough to pick any random schema whereof S is an instance and then test it for validity. If the schema proves to be valid, then we do know that S is truth-functionally true; but if the schema does not prove to be valid we cannot conclude that S is not truth-functionally true, for S might still be an instance of some other schema which *is* valid. The statement (1), e.g., is an instance of '$\sim(p\bar{q})$', also of '$\sim(pq)$', also of '$\bar{p}$', and also of 'p'; yet the nonvalidity of these schemata does not alter the fact that (1) is truth-functionally true. But if from among the various schemata whereof S is an instance we pick the most detailed sort—'$\sim(p\bar{p})$' in the case of (1)—then a test of validity of this schema does decide whether or not S is truth-functionally true. We must pick a schema which reflects the whole truth-functional structure of S. This is done by putting letters for only the simple components of S, and the same letter for all occurrences of the same simple component, so that the letters answer exactly to the simple components.

But instead of supplanting simple components thus by corresponding letters and subjecting the result to the validity test, we might as well apply the latter technique directly to the original statement—manipulating the constituent simple statements instead of the corresponding letters. Thus we have, parallel to the formulation in §23, the following *test of truth-functional truth*. Translate the statement into terms of '~', 'v', and '.', and transform the whole into conjunctional normal form. If the result is an alternation which exhibits both a statement and its denial, it is truth-functionally true. If it is a conjunction purely of such alternations, again it is truth-functionally true. And otherwise it is not truth-functionally true, though it may still be true. Let us test, e.g., the statement:

(2)   If Jones is ill then Smith is away unless Jones is ill and Smith is not away.

Let us use abbreviations 'J' and 'S' for the simple statements 'Jones is ill' and 'Smith is away';

If J then S unless J and not S.

Translated step by step according to § 13 and other sections, this becomes successively:

$$\sim(J \,.\, \sim S \text{ unless } J \text{ and not } S),$$

$$\sim(J \,.\, \sim(S \text{ v } J \text{ and not } S)),$$

$$\sim(J \,.\, \sim(S \text{ v } (J \,.\, \text{not } S))),$$

(3) $\sim(J \,.\, \sim(S \text{ v } (J \,.\, \sim S))).$

(In these translations we have assumed that the 'unless' of (2) was supposed to govern the whole 'and' compound, and that the 'then' was supposed to govern the whole 'unless' compound.) Then we convert (3) to conjunctional normal form.

$$\sim J \text{ v } S \text{ v } (J \,.\, \sim S) \qquad \qquad §21(13)$$

$$\sim J \text{ v } S \text{ v } J \,.\, \sim J \text{ v } S \text{ v } \sim S. \qquad §21(3)$$

This meets the criterion of truth-functional truth.

Again we could have accelerated matters by simplifying early. (3) simplifies by §21(12) to '$\sim(J \,.\, \sim(S \text{ v } J))$', i.e., by §21(13), '$\sim J \text{ v } S \text{ v } J$'.

Exercises

1. Test the statement in Exercise 4 of §22 for truth-functional truth.

2. Test these statements for truth-functional truth:

> If Jones will not come unless Smith does, nor will Smith unless Robinson does, then Robinson will come if Jones does.

> If Jones envies Smith or vice versa, but they do not envy each other, then Jones envies Smith if and only if Smith does not envy Jones.

§ 25. Inconsistency and Truth-Functional Falsity

A schema whose instances are all false is called inconsistent. E.g., each of the schemata §16(2) is inconsistent. Many schemata are of course neither valid nor inconsistent; viz., those that have some true instances and some false ones.

What was argued in §23 with regard to validity can be argued for inconsistency in exactly parallel fashion, just switching 'true' with 'false' and conjunction with alternation. We see thus that *a schema is inconsistent if it is derived by substitution in an inconsistent schema;* also that *one of two equivalent schemata is inconsistent if and only if the other is;* and finally that *an alternational normal schema is inconsistent if and only if it either is a conjunction in which one literal denies another, or else is an alternation of such conjunctions.*

To test the inconsistency of:

(1) $p \vee q \cdot \bar{q} \vee \bar{r} \cdot \bar{p}r,$

e.g., we may transform the schema into an alternational normal schema thus:

$$(p \vee q \cdot \bar{q}) \vee (p \vee_{\scriptscriptstyle \iota} \cdot \bar{r}) \cdot \bar{p}r \qquad \S21(10)$$

$$p\bar{q} \vee q\bar{q} \vee p\bar{r} \vee q\bar{r} \cdot \bar{p}r \qquad \S21(10)$$

$$p\bar{q}\bar{p}r \vee q\bar{q}\bar{p}r \vee p\bar{r}\bar{p}r \vee q\bar{r}\bar{p}r \qquad \S21(10)$$

This meets the criterion of inconsistency.

As usual we could do better by simplifying early. Rearranged, (1) is '$p \lor q \cdot \bar{p} \cdot \bar{q} \lor \bar{r} \cdot r$'; but '$p \lor q \cdot \bar{p}$' becomes '$\bar{p}q$' by §21(5), and '$\bar{q} \lor \bar{r} \cdot r$' becomes '$r\bar{q}$' by the same; so we have '$\bar{p}qr\bar{q}$'.

Valid schemata go into inconsistent ones both under denial and under duality. *A schema is inconsistent if and only if its denial is valid;* for the instances of the one schema are the denials of the instances of the other, and hence are all false if and only if the instances of the other are all true. At the same time *a schema is inconsistent if and only if its dual is valid.* For, the truth table of the one schema is that of the other with 'T' and '⊥' switched throughout (cf. §21); hence all its rows are marked '⊥' if and only if all rows of the other are marked 'T'.

A statement will be called *truth-functionally false* when it is an instance of an inconsistent truth-functional schema or when it is such as to become an instance of an inconsistent truth-functional schema on translation into terms of '∼', '∨' and '·'. The statement:

(2)   Jones is ill . ∼ Jones is ill

is truth-functionally false, being an instance of the inconsistent schema '$p\bar{p}$'. Likewise the statement:

Jones is ill but Jones is not ill

is truth-functionally false, since it gives way to (2) when translated according to §§ 3–6. A truth-functionally false statement is one which is false by virtue merely of its structure in terms of truth-functions; it remains false when its constituent simple statements are varied at will. A statement is truth-functionally false if and only if its denial is truth-functionally true.

To test a statement for truth-functional falsity, then, we translate it into terms of '∼', '∨', and '·', and transform the whole into alternational normal form. If the result is a conjunction which exhibits both a statement and its denial, it is truth-functionally false. If it is an alternation purely of such conjunctions, again it is truth-functionally false. And otherwise it is not truth-functionally false, though it still may be false.

Exercises

1. Test this schema for inconsistency:

$$\sim(pq) \cdot \sim(p\bar{q}) \cdot \sim(\bar{p}q) \cdot \sim(\bar{p}\bar{q}).$$

2. Test these statements for truth-functional falsity:

>If Britain wins, so will France; moreover, Britain or France will win, but they will not both win.

>Britain will win if and only if Italy does not win; but both Britain and Italy will win.

§ 26. Implication between Schemata

One schema will be said to *imply* another if these respective schemata have no corresponding instances such that the first is true and the second is false. The schema 'pq', e.g., implies 'p'. For, where S_1 and S_2 are corresponding instances of the respective schemata, S_1 is a conjunction of two statements one of which is S_2; hence S_1 will not be true if S_2 is false.

One schema implies another just in case the conjunction of the one schema with the denial of the other is inconsistent. Briefly, the one implies the other when it is "inconsistent with" the other's denial. The implication of 'p' by 'pq', e.g., amounts to the inconsistency of '$pq\bar{p}$'. This principle is established as follows. The instances of a conjunction of two schemata comprise all and only those statements which are conjunctions of corresponding instances of the two component schemata (disregarding order). Hence the conjunctive schema will have a true instance just in case the two component schemata have a pair of corresponding instances both of which are true. Thus the conjunctive schema will be inconsistent if and only if the two component schemata have no pair of corresponding instances both of which are true. Then, where the component schemata are S_1 and the denial of S_2, the conjunctive schema is inconsistent just in case S_1 and the denial of S_2 have no pair of corresponding instances both of which are true; in other words, just in case S_1 and S_2 have no pair of corresponding instances such that the first is true and the second is false. But this is what we mean by saying that S_1 implies S_2.

Thus, to decide whether one schema implies another, we have only to deny the second schema, conjoin it with the first, and test the result for inconsistency by the method noted in §25. To discover, e.g., that '$p \vee q \cdot \bar{q} \vee \bar{r}$' implies '$\sim(\bar{p}r)$', we test:

$$p \vee q \cdot \bar{q} \vee \bar{r} \cdot \sim\sim(\bar{p}r),$$

i.e. §25(1), for inconsistency—as has been done.

Comparison of the definition of implication with that of equivalence (§16) shows that *equivalence is mutual implication;* two schemata are equivalent if and only if they imply each other. Equivalence can be tested, therefore, simply by two tests of implication in the above manner. There is indeed a less cumbersome way of establishing the equivalence of two schemata, viz. simply through transformation of the one schema into the other by §16(1)–(6); it was in this way that we established the various equivalences of §20. But this method lacks the character of a mechanical *test*. Discovery of the particular series of steps of transformation by §16(1)–(6) which leads from a schema S_1 to a schema S_2 is a hit-and-miss matter; we might fail to discover the appropriate series of steps even though it exists. Thus, whereas discovery of such a series does establish the equivalence of S_1 and S_2, mere failure to discover such a series gives us no assurance that S_1 and S_2 are not equivalent. On the other hand our newly formulated test of equivalence, like the tests of implication, validity, and inconsistency, leads methodically and unfailingly to a final decision—affirmative or negative—in every case.

Exercise

Among the following five schemata, which imply which?

$$p, \qquad pq, \qquad \sim(\bar{p}\bar{q}), \qquad p \vee p\bar{q}, \qquad q \cdot \sim(\bar{p}q).$$

(This exercise should be used selectively if twenty tests of implication seem excessive.)

§ 27. Truth-Functional Implication

One statement is said to *imply* another *truth-functionally* (cf. §14) if the respective statements are corresponding instances of truth-functional schemata such that the one schema implies the other. Or, what comes to the same thing in view of §26, one statement truth-functionally implies another if the conjunction of the one statement with the denial of the other is truth-functionally false. In view of §25, accordingly, we have the following test for truth-functional implication. Given two statements, we first translate them into terms of '$\sim$', 'v', and '.'; then we conjoin the one statement with the denial of the other and convert to alternational normal form (simultaneously simplifying, if we like). If the result is a conjunction which, or an alternation of conjunctions each of which, exhibits both a statement and its denial, then the first of the original statements truth-functionally implies the second; otherwise not.

To see, e.g., that the statement:

(1)　　　Robinson is responsible unless Jones and Smith were there

truth-functionally implies the statement:

(2)　　　If Jones was not there, Robinson is responsible,

we first translate these into:

(3)　　　　　　　　　R v (J . S),

(4)　　　　　　　　　$\sim$($\sim$J . $\sim$R)

where 'R', 'J', and 'S' are short for 'Robinson is responsible', 'Jones was there', and 'Smith was there'. Then we conjoin (3) with the denial of (4), thus:

R v (J . S) . $\sim$J . $\sim$R

(cancelling a double denial in the process). The part 'R v (J . S) . $\sim$R' here simplifies to '$\sim$R . J . S' by §21(5), so the whole becomes '$\sim$R . J . S . $\sim$J'. This reveals that (1) implies (2).

Just as equivalence of schemata is mutual implication (cf. §26), so truth-functional equivalence of statements is mutual truth-functional implication. Accordingly we can test truth-functional equivalence by testing two truth-functional implications in the above manner.

When we test truth-functional implication, we are testing whether the one statement follows from the other by virtue solely of the structure of the two statements in terms of truth functions. To say that one statement truth-functionally implies another is not merely to deny that the statements are respectively true and false, but to deny further that there are *any* two statements which are like the given ones in truth-functional structure and are respectively true and false. (See §17 for parallel remarks on truth-functional equivalence.)

The reader is perhaps tempted at this point to regard truth-functional implication as a strong conditional—one which brings its two components into more intimate connection than does the truth-functional conditional of §7. It may appear, accordingly, that we have departed from our policy (§9) of dealing with none but truth-functional modes of statement composition. This, however, is a confusion. When we say that one statement truth-functionally implies another (or that they are truth-functionally equivalent) we are talking *about* the statements—and about their structure with regard to truth-functional modes of composition. The statement:

(1) truth-functionally implies (2)

is not itself a compound of the statements (1) and (2), nor indeed does it contain those statements; it contains names *of* them, viz. '(1)' and '(2)', and thereby talks *about* the statements (1) and (2). On the other hand the statement (2) is genuinely a compound of the statements 'Jones was not there' and 'Robinson is responsible'; (2) contains those statements, and talks not *about* those statements but about Jones and Robinson. 'If . . . then' is a connective of statements, but 'truth-functionally implies' is not; it is a transitive verb, a connective of nouns, in particular a connective of names of statements.[1]

Exercises

1. Among the following statements, which truth-functionally imply which?

Jones will come,

Jones will come unless Smith urges him,

Smith will not urge Jones, but Jones will come,

Jones will come only if Smith urges him, but Smith will urge him.

2. Which of these statements are truth-functionally equivalent? Prove each equivalence by translating the statements into terms of

[1] Cf. *Mathematical Logic*, §§ 4–5; also Alfred Tarski, *Introduction to Logic* (New York, 1941), pp. 29–32, and Rudolf Carnap, *Logical Syntax of Language* (New York and London, 1937), pp. 153–60, 245–60.

conjunction and denial, using abbreviations as in §10, and then transforming the one statement into the other.

> The rest of the inhabitants will emigrate if there is a drought or a hurricane this year.

> The rest of the inhabitants will emigrate if there is a drought this year, or the rest of the inhabitants will emigrate if there is a hurricane this year.

> The rest of the inhabitants will emigrate if there are a drought and a hurricane this year.

> The rest of the inhabitants will emigrate if there is a drought this year, and the rest of the inhabitants will emigrate if there is a hurricane this year.

> If there is a drought this year, then if there is a hurricane this year the rest of the inhabitants will emigrate.

3. Repeat the exercise making, in each case, two implication tests.

III • QUANTIFICATION

§ 28. 'Something'

THUS FAR we have been analyzing statements only into component statements. Those having no component statements have accordingly stood as the limits of analysis. But now we are ready to break into these latter statements, directing our attention to component expressions other than statements. These further analyses center around idioms involving the word 'something' and related locutions.

The true statements:

(1)   London is big and noisy,

(2)   London is big and London is noisy

are obviously just two ways of saying the same thing; and both go into symbols as the conjunction:

London is big . London is noisy

of the two true statements 'London is big' and 'London is noisy'. Similarly the false statements:

(3)   London is big and small,

(4)   London is big and London is small

are just two ways of writing the conjunction:

London is big . London is small

of the truth 'London is big' and the falsehood 'London is small'. On the other hand the statements:

(5)   Something is big and small,

(6)   Something is big and something is small

are *not* just two ways of saying the same thing. (6) amounts indeed to the conjunction:

Something is big . something is small

of the true statements 'Something is big' and 'Something is small', and is accordingly true: but (5), far from being translatable into this true conjunction, is false.

The outward similarity which (5)–(6) bear to (1)–(2) and to (3)–(4) is thus deceptive. The logic of such statements as (5)–(6) is clarified by switching over to a more elaborate idiom:

(7)   There is something such that it is big and small,

(8)   There is something such that it is big and there is something such that it is small.

The misleading resemblance of (5) to (1) and (3) drops out in the case of (7). What resembles (1) and (3) is not (7) as a whole, but its part:

(9)   it is big and small.

This degree of resemblance is quite unobjectionable; for the part (9) *can* quite properly be expanded as:

(10)   it is big and it is small,

just as (1) can be expanded as (2) and (3) as (4). We can quite properly paraphrase (7) as:

(11)   There is something such that it is big and it is small,

which, however, remains essentially different from (6) and (8). Whereas (11) consists of a prefix 'there is something such that' followed by an expression (10) which has the form of a conjunction, on the other hand (8) is a conjunction of two statements each of which begins with a prefix of that kind.

As a step toward a compact notation, let us write '∃' for 'there is'. Thus (11) becomes:

(12)   ∃ something such that (it is big . it is small),

whereas (8) becomes:

(13)   ∃ something such that it is big . ∃ something such that it is small.

(12) amounts to (11) and to (7) and (5), and is false; on the other hand (13) amounts to (8) and to (6), and is true.

Exercise

To what extent can the foregoing reflections on 'something' be adapted to 'nothing'? to 'everything'? Scrutinize each detail, in expectation of a breach of analogy here and there.

§ 29. Quantifiers

In order to say that what:

(1)   Boston is far from London

says of London is true of something, we would ordinarily put 'something' for 'London' and get:

(2)   Boston is far from something.

But the symbolic method, as of §28, is rather this: we put 'it' for 'London' in (1) and apply the prefix 'Ǝ something such that', getting:

(3)   Ǝ something such that Boston is far from it.

Similarly, in order to say that what (2) says of Boston is true of something, we would put 'something' for 'Boston' and get:

(4)   Something is far from something.

Or, under the symbolic method, we would put 'it' for 'Boston' in (2) and apply the prefix 'Ǝ something such that', getting:

(5)   Ǝ something such that it is far from something.

But the part:

(6)   it is far from something,

in (5), still wants translation into symbols. To see how to do this, we refer back to the symbolic translation (3) of (2). Since (6) is like (2) except for having 'it' in place of 'Boston', the proper symbolic translation of (6) would seem to be (3) with 'it' in place of 'Boston':

(7)   Ǝ something such that it is far from it.

Then, putting (7) for (6) in (5), we get the following fully symbolic rendering of (5):

(8)   Ǝ something such that Ǝ something such that it is far from it.

But this is obviously unsatisfactory, for the distinction is lost between the 'it' which corresponds to the first 'something' and the 'it' which corresponds to the second 'something'. We might remove this difficulty by applying arbitrary numerical subscripts to 'something' and 'it'. (3) and (5) might be rendered respectively:

(9)   ∃ something$_2$ such that Boston is far from it$_2$,

(10)   ∃ something$_1$ such that it$_1$ is far from something.

Now the part:

(11)   it$_1$ is far from something

of (10) differs from (2) only in exhibiting 'it$_1$' in place of 'Boston'; and accordingly, just as (2) goes into symbols as (9), so (11) goes into symbols as:

(12)   ∃ something$_2$ such that it$_1$ is far from it$_2$.

Then, putting (12) for (11) in (10), we get:

(13)   ∃ something$_1$ such that ∃ something$_2$ such that it$_1$ is far from it$_2$

as the full symbolic rendering of (10) (and of (4)). This result is free from the defect noted in (8).

Such use of distinguishing subscripts corresponds to the common use of 'former' and 'latter'. (13) might be set over literally into words thus:

There is something such that there is something such that the former is far from the latter.

It is usual to condense this notation by writing '(∃x)', '(∃y)', etc. instead of '∃ something such that' with different subscripts, and then using the same letter again instead of 'it' with the corresponding subscript. Thus revised, (9) and (13) become:

(14)   (∃x) Boston is far from x,

(15)   (∃y)(∃x) y is far from x;

similarly §28(12)–(13) become:

(16)   (∃x)(x is big . x is small),

(17)   (∃x) x is big . (∃y) y is small.

This last could indeed be rendered just as well thus:

(18)   (∃x) x is big . (∃x) x is small;

the need of distinct letters arises only in cases such as (15).

74

The prefixes '(∃x)', '(∃y)', etc. are called *quantifiers;* and the construction of statements with their help is called quantification. Also a statement so formed will be called a quantification. A quantifier is conveniently read in the fashion 'there is something *x* such that'; thus (15) may be read 'there is something *y* such that there is something *x* such that *y* is far from *x*'.

Exercises

Translate these statements into the notation of quantification and conjunction:

>Sadie stole something at the Emporium,

>Sadie stole something at the Emporium but returned it,

>Sadie stole something at the Emporium and exchanged it for something.

§ 30. Variables and Open Sentences

The occurrence of '*x*' in '(∃x)' answers, we have seen, to 'something' or 'something such that'; and the recurrences of '*x*' subsequent to '(∃x)' answer to occurrences of 'it' referring back to 'something'. As usual '*x*' will be called a *variable;* and similarly for '*y*', '*z*', etc. So as never to run short of variables, we may form new ones by use of accents; thus the variables will be taken as '*u*', '*v*', '*w*', '*x*', '*y*', '*z*', '*u'*', '*v'*', '*u''*', etc.

Variables bear little analogy to statement letters. Whereas statement letters occur in positions appropriate to statements, variables do not; they occur rather in positions of the kind appropriate to nouns and pronouns—cf. 'far from *x*', also '*x* is big'. Moreover, variables occur also in quantifiers, whereas statement letters do not. Another essential difference is that whereas statement letters occur in schemata but never in statements, variables occur directly in statements; e.g. '*x*' occurs in the statement §29(14), which is the symbolic equivalent of the statement §29(2).

But a variable cannot occur in a statement unless a quantifier is present. The part '*x* is big' of §29(16), e.g., is no statement, but only

75

a fragment of one or another statement such as §29(16)–(18). Fragments of this kind will be called *open sentences;* thus an open sentence is an expression which is not a statement but can be turned into a statement by applying one or more quantifiers. The open sentence '*x* is big', e.g., can be turned into the statement '(∃*x*) *x* is big' by applying '(∃*x*)'. The open sentence:

(1)   *x* is big . *x* is small

can be turned into the statement §29(16) by applying '(∃*x*)'. (Application of the quantifier involves attachment of parentheses here, because of the conjunction.) The open sentence:

(2)   (∃*x*) *y* is far from *x*

can be turned into the statement §29(15) by applying '(∃*y*)'. The open sentence:

(3)   *y* is far from *x*

can be turned into the statement §29(15) by successively applying the two quantifiers '(∃*x*)' and '(∃*y*)'.

An open sentence always has the form of a statement, but exhibits variables not governed by quantifiers. The analogue of an open sentence in ordinary language would exhibit 'it', or 'the former' and 'the latter', etc., in place of those variables (cf. §29). Thus '*x* is big' answers to the words 'it is big'; again (2) answers to the words 'it is far from something'; and (3) answers to the words 'the former is far from the latter'. The variable having no associated quantifier thus reappears in words as a dangling pronoun—a pronoun in want of an antecedent. Sentences containing such pronouns answer to open sentences.

There are, of course, idioms in which 'it' calls for no antecedent—e.g. 'it is raining'; and there are circumstances where the intended antecedent of the pronoun may be tacitly understood—e.g. in saying 'it is steep' on the brink of El Capitan. In such ways, genuine statements or elliptical indications of statements are capable of containing 'it' without an expressed antecedent. Considered apart from any such tacit antecedent, however, the sentences 'it is steep', 'it is far from something', 'the former is far from the latter', etc. obviously affirm nothing, and are not statements at all; they are mere fragments, capable of being woven into longer expressions which are statements as wholes. Such fragments as these are the verbal prototypes of open sentences.

Since all forms which statements can take on are available equally to open sentences, an open sentence may in particular have the form of a denial—e.g. '~ *x* is big'. Likewise an open sentence may be a conjunction, e.g. (1), or a quantification, e.g. (2). Thus denial is no longer describable merely as turning statements into statements, but rather as turning statements into statements and open sentences into open sentences. Similarly conjunction not only joins statements to form a statement, but it may also join open sentences, or a statement and an open sentence, to form an open sentence. Moreover, quantification yields statements *or* open sentences: it applies to (1) to yield the statement §29(16), and to (3) to yield the open sentence (2).

Quantifiers in certain positions raise questions of interpretation. What are we to make of the following forms?

(4) $(\exists x)(x$ is a city . $(\exists x)$ x is big),

(5) $(\exists x)$ Socrates is mortal,

(6) $(\exists x)$ y is mortal.

We could ban them by imposing certain grammatical restrictions on the use of quantifiers. But an easier course is to keep our grammar simple and adopt supplementary conventions of interpretation for puzzling cases. In (4), where '$(\exists x)$' governs an open sentence in which '$(\exists x)$' reappears, the 'x' of 'x is big' could evidently refer back to either the remoter or the nearer '$(\exists x)$'; and the best convention to adopt is that it refer back to the nearer. Thus (4) may be read simply as:

$(\exists x)(x$ is a city . $(\exists y)$ y is big),

i.e., 'There is something such that it is a city and something is big'.

As for (5) and (6), the best convention is that a quantifier be treated as idle and vacuous when its variable does not recur. Thus (5) is taken as amounting simply to the statement 'Socrates is mortal', and (6) to the open sentence 'y is mortal'.

Exercises

1. Which of the following are statements? Which are open sentences? One is neither.

$(\exists x)($Tom traded x for y . $p)$,

$(\exists x)($Tom traded x for y . Tom lost $y)$,

77

$(\exists x)((\exists y)$ Tom traded x for y . Tom lost y),

$(\exists x)(\exists y)$(Tom traded x for y . Tom lost y),

$(\exists x)((\exists y)$ Tom traded x for y . $(\exists y)$ Tom lost y),

$(\exists y)((\exists x)$ Tom traded x for y . Tom lost y).

Justify each of your answers.

2. Translate each statement and each open sentence of Exercise 1 into as concise and natural a verbal formulation as you can.

§ 31. Variants of 'Some'

We have seen that the quantifier answers to the verbal idiom 'there is something such that', and that recurrences of the variable answer to 'it'. This verbal idiom has variants which have the same meaning, e.g. 'there is a thing such that', 'there is at least one thing such that'. Synonyms such as 'object' or 'entity' may appear instead of 'thing', and 'exists' may appear instead of 'is'. Also these idioms may, without change of meaning, give way to plural forms—'there are one or more things such that', 'one or more entities exist such that', etc. They may be rendered simply 'there are some things such that', 'there are things such that', 'entities exist such that', etc., provided that these are understood in the sense 'there are one or more' rather than 'there are two or more'. The notation of quantification developed in §§28–30 answers indifferently to all these verbal variants, and, as we shall see, to further ones as well.

The combination 'such that it' or 'such that they' is commonly condensed to 'that'. Instead of saying 'There is something such that it cures malaria', we would commonly say:

(1)   There is something that cures malaria.

The combination 'something such that it is', when followed by a substantive, is commonly omitted altogether; instead, e.g., of saying 'There is something such that it is a five-legged calf', or 'Something such that it is a five-legged calf exists', we would say simply 'There is a five-legged calf', 'A five-legged calf exists'. The corresponding plural idioms 'things such that they are', 'entities such that they are', etc. are likewise commonly omitted when followed by substantives; instead, e.g., of saying 'There are some things such that they are five-legged calves', or 'Things such that they are five-legged calves exist', we would say simply:

(2)   There are some five-legged calves.

(3)   Five-legged calves exist.

But the symbolism remains uniform:

(4) $(\exists x)$ x cures malaria,

(5) $(\exists x)$ x is a five-legged calf.

Incidentally the latter may be analyzed a little more:

(6) $(\exists x)(x$ is five-legged $.$ x is a calf$)$.

There are many ways of translating quantifications into words; or, viewing the matter from the other end, there are many idioms which give way uniformly to quantifications when rendered into symbols. Besides the considerable variety of idioms noted just now, we must count in the idiom originally noted in §28(5)–(6), §29(2), and §29(4); it consists in using 'something' as a straight substantive in the body of the statement, unaccompanied by 'there is' or 'exists' or 'it'. Also this idiom has minor variants. Instead of 'something' we may use 'some object', 'some entity', 'at least one thing', etc.; and, as in the contexts previously considered, we may switch over to plural forms without any alteration of meaning. All these usages are translatable into symbols in precisely the manner in which §28(5)–(6), §29(2), and §29(4) were translated into §29(14)–(18); viz., by putting a variable in place of 'something' or its equivalent and prefixing a quantifier.

Exercise

See in how many additional ways you can do Exercise 2 of §30 in view of the present section.

§ 32. 'Some' Restricted

There is another important set of idioms which is precisely like the set considered in §31 except that the words 'thing', 'object', 'entity', etc. give way to more restrictive terms such as 'city', 'calf', etc. Parallel to §29(2), e.g., there is the more specific statement:

(1)   Boston is far from some city.

This can be paraphrased as:

> There is something such that it is a city and Boston is far
> from it,

and hence goes into symbols thus:

(2)   ($\exists x$)(x is a city . Boston is far from x).

The translation (2) of (1) differs from the translation §29(14) of
§29(2) only in that 'x is a city' is inserted in conjunction. Similarly,
whereas 'Something is five-legged' goes into symbols as:

> ($\exists x$) x is five-legged,

'Some calf is five-legged' goes into symbols rather as:

> ($\exists x$)(x is a calf . x is five-legged),

and is just another way of saying that there is a five-legged calf
(cf. §31(6)).

Occasionally 'some' in such positions is supplanted simply by
'a'—e.g., 'I wrote a poem', symbolically:

(3)   ($\exists x$)(x is a poem . I wrote x).

But we cannot in general depend upon 'a' to carry the sense of
'some'. When I say 'I loathe a liar' I am likely to mean, not merely
that there is at least one liar whom I happen to loathe, but rather
that I loathe every liar. In these connections, as in the case of statement composition (cf. §§5, 11), there is little hope of drawing up
complete and unfailing rules for the translation of words into symbols; we must continue in some degree to guess intentions.

What is accomplished by putting a restrictive noun for the 'thing'
of 'something', as in (1), is commonly accomplished also by keeping
'something' but restricting it by adding an adjective. An example is
'Something good is in the box', which goes into symbols as:

(4)   ($\exists x$)(x is good . x is in the box);

again 'Something big is small' goes into symbols as §29(16). Or, instead of an adjective, we commonly use a 'which' or 'that' clause or
an adjective phrase. Thus the statement:

(5)   Something that lays eggs suckles its young

goes into symbols as:

$$(\exists x)(x \text{ lays eggs} \cdot x \text{ suckles its young}).$$

Similarly the statement:

(6)   There is something in my kit that cures malaria,

formed by insertion of an adjective phrase in §31(1), goes into symbols as:

$$(\exists x)(x \text{ is in my kit} \cdot x \text{ cures malaria}).$$

The foregoing devices commonly occur also in combination. E.g., we may supplant the 'thing' of (5) by a more restrictive term 'biped', getting:

(7)   Some biped that lays eggs suckles its young,

which goes into symbols as:

(8) $(\exists x)(x \text{ is a biped} \cdot x \text{ lays eggs} \cdot x \text{ suckles its young}).$

Or, inserting 'Australian' after 'something' in (5), we get a statement which goes into symbols as:

$$(\exists x)(x \text{ is Australian} \cdot x \text{ lays eggs} \cdot x \text{ suckles its young}).$$

The 'some' of these idioms can, as in the idioms of §31, be rendered alternatively as 'at least one'; also 'a certain'. All these idioms admit also of being put into the plural without change of meaning. E.g., 'Some calf is five-legged' can just as well be phrased 'One or more calves are five-legged', or simply 'Some calves are five-legged' provided that we understand the plural 'some' as meaning 'one or more' rather than 'two or more'. Similarly (7) could be phrased 'Some bipeds that lay eggs suckle their young'. Commonly, also, 'some' in application thus to a plural noun is idly elaborated into 'some of the'.

Exercises

1. See in how many further ways you can do the preceding exercise in view of this section.

2. Paraphrase the following into a quantification of a conjunction of seven open sentences:

> I was carrying and scrutinizing a square green package the origin and contents of which were altogether unknown to me.

§ 33. 'No'

When a statement involves 'some' (or in particular 'something'), attachment of 'not' to its main verb does not in general produce a denial of the statement (cf. §4). Ordinarily it produces merely another statement of the 'some' type, rather than the denial of a statement of that type. E.g., 'Something does not bore George' is not the denial of 'Something bores George'. Whereas the latter goes into symbols as:

(1) $(\exists x)$ x bores George,

the former does not express the denial:

(2) $\sim(\exists x)$ x bores George;

it expresses rather another quantification:

(3) $(\exists x)\sim$ x bores George

to the effect that there are at least some things in the world that do not bore George. (1) and (3), far from being denials the one of the other, are probably both true.

The ordinary method of denying 'Something bores George' consists rather in changing 'some' to 'no'; thus (2) is the symbolic rendering of 'Nothing bores George'. Similarly each of the 'some' idioms of foregoing sections can be denied simply by changing 'some' to 'no'. To deny §28(5) we say 'Nothing is big and small'; to deny §32(1) we say 'Boston is far from no city'; to deny §31(2) we say 'There are no five-legged calves'; to deny §32(7) we say 'No biped that lays eggs suckles its young'. Symbolically:

(4) $\sim(\exists x)(x$ is big . x is small),

(5) $\sim(\exists x)(x$ is a city . Boston is far from x),

(6) $\sim(\exists x)(x$ is five-legged . x is a calf),

(7) $\sim(\exists x)(x$ is a biped . x lays eggs . x suckles its young).

The notation of quantification enables us thus to translate not merely all the 'some' idioms of foregoing sections but also a precisely parallel array of 'no' idioms. The symbolic difference between the two sets of idioms consists only of an initial denial sign.

Just as '(∃x)' is read 'there is something x such that', so the combination of signs '∼(∃x)' as in (2) and (4)–(7) may be read 'there is nothing x such that'. Just as a statement such as (1) is true if and only if the part following '(∃x)' is true for *some* entity (thought of as named in the position of 'x'), so a statement such as (2) or (4)–(7) is true if and only if the part following '∼(∃x)' is true for *no* entity—false for *every* entity. On the other hand a statement such as (3) is true if and only if the part following '(∃x)∼' is false for some entity. Of course the signs in '∼(∃x)' or '(∃x)∼' do not actually hang together as a self-contained unit; the '∼' in (2) applies in no sense to '(∃x)' but to (1) as a whole, and the '(∃x)' in (3) applies in no sense to '∼' but to '∼x bores George' as a whole.

Replacement of 'some' by 'no' is by no means the only idiomatic way of denying the 'some' idiom. We have seen that mere negation of the main verb fails to produce a denial of a 'some' statement; but it does often succeed if accompanied by a change of 'some' to 'any'. 'Boston is not far from any city', e.g., is as good a reading of (5) as 'Boston is far from no city'; and 'There are not any five-legged calves' is as good a reading of (6) as 'There are no five-legged calves'. We observed that 'Something does not bore George' is not the denial of 'Something bores George', and now we observe further that 'Boston is not far from any city' is the denial not of 'Boston is far from any city' but of 'Boston is far from some city'. (See also below, §35.)

The verbal rendering of such statements as (2) and (4)–(7) need not always involve 'no' or 'not . . . any', any more than the statements which they deny always involve 'some'. Since, e.g., §31(6) may appear in words not only as §31(2) but alternatively as §31(3), it follows that its denial (6) above may appear in words alternatively as the denial:

Five-legged calves do not exist

of §31(3). Attachment of 'not' to the verb fails to yield the denial when 'some' appears, as remarked, but it serves quite well in application to forms such as §31(3) which do not use 'some'. Of course a statement of *any* form can be denied, rather artificially, by applying 'it is not the case that' to the whole (cf. §4); so a whole broad array of further readings of such statements as (2) and (4)–(7) is obtainable simply by applying 'it is not the case that' to any of the idioms considered in §§31–32.

Exercises

1. Deny each of the *statements* in Exercise 1, §30, and translate these denials into idiomatic English using in each case some idiom involving 'no'.

2. Translate these into symbols as completely as possible:

> None of my leather-bound books from the fifteenth century is as well preserved as this Plutarch.

> There is no Renaissance poem more simply expressed and yet none more difficult to interpret than the "Hymeneal Hymn" of Pedaccio.

§ 34. 'Every'

The statement §33(3) says that there are some things that do not bore George; hence if we prefer to say that everything bores George, we have only to deny §33(3):

(1) $\sim(\exists x)\sim x$ bores George.

Again, the statement:

(2) $(\exists x)\sim x$ is x

says that there is something that is not itself; accordingly, if we want to deny this falsehood and affirm rather that everything is itself, we write:

(3) $\sim(\exists x)\sim x$ is x.

'Everything' may occur restricted in the various ways noted in the case of 'something', and it may occur unrestricted as in 'Everything bores George', 'Everything is itself'. Just as the unrestricted use of 'something' is translated into symbols by putting 'x' (or 'y', etc.) for 'something' and applying '$(\exists x)$' (or '$(\exists y)$' etc.), as observed in §29, so the unrestricted use of 'everything' is translated into symbols by putting 'x' for 'everything' and applying '$\sim(\exists x)\sim$'. Just as '$(\exists x)$' is read 'there is something x such that', and '$\sim(\exists x)$' is read 'there is nothing x such that' (cf. §33), so '$\sim(\exists x)\sim$' may be read 'no matter what x may be'. A statement such as (1) or (3) is true just in case what the part following '$\sim(\exists x)\sim$' affirms of x is true of every entity—false of none. Of course, the signs in ' $\sim$ ($\exists x$) $\sim$ ' do not hang together as a self-contained unit; the first '$\sim$' in (3) applies in no sense to '($\exists x$)' or to '($\exists x$)$\sim$' but to (2) as a whole, and the '($\exists x$)' in (3) applies to '$\sim x$ is x' as a whole.

Restriction of 'something' by adding an adjectival word or phrase or a relative clause, or by supplanting 'thing' by a new substantive, has been seen (§32) to amount in logical notation to the insertion of a suitable restrictive clause conjunctively after the quantifier. Restriction of 'everything' is analogous. E.g., we may restrict 'Everything bores George' by inserting the relative clause 'that interests me', or by supplanting 'thing' by 'outdoor sport'; and we can achieve the same effect in symbols by inserting 'x interests me' or 'x is an outdoor sport' conjunctively after the '($\exists x$)' of (1). The statements:

(4)   Everything that interests me bores George,

(5)   Every outdoor sport bores George

become:

(6) $\sim$($\exists x$)(x interests me $.\ \sim x$ bores George),

(7) $\sim$($\exists x$)(x is an outdoor sport $.\ \sim x$ bores George).

For (4) amounts to saying that there is nothing which interests me and yet fails to bore George; and this takes on the symbolic form (6) in view of §33. Correspondingly for (5).

Often, of course, the words by which 'everything' is supposed to be restricted are in practice simply left tacit in the belief that the hearer is in position to supply them for himself. E.g. the words 'Everything came by express' would be accepted as a partial utterance of some statement of the type (6)–(7) rather than as a trivial falsehood of the type (1). But equally elliptic usage is common in connection with the idioms considered in earlier sections; when one says 'There is something in the box', e.g., he is likely to mean 'something which is not air, dust, etc.'.

Exercise

Which of the following statements become indistinguishable from one another on translation into symbols?

Every man is mortal,

Everything that is a man is mortal,

Everything is either not a man or else mortal,

Nothing is a man and yet not mortal,

It is not the case that some men are not mortal,

No man is not mortal,

There are no men that are not mortal.

§ 35. Variants of 'Every'

Parallel to what was noted in the case of 'something' (§31), we may say 'every object', 'every entity', etc. instead of 'everything'. Also, parallel to what was observed in the case of 'some' (§31), we may switch over to plural forms without change of meaning—using 'all' or 'all the' instead of 'every'. Thus §34(3) may be read 'Every entity is itself', 'All things are themselves', 'All objects are themselves'; and §34(6) may be read 'All things that interest me bore George', or 'All the things that interest me bore George'. Again the statement:

(1)   Smith can outplay every member of the team,

symbolically:

(2) $\sim(\exists x)(x$ is a member of the team $.\ \sim$ Smith can outplay $x)$,

can be rephrased:

(3)   Smith can outplay all the members of the team.

However, (3) illustrates an ambiguity that does sometimes arise in the use of 'all'; for we cannot be quite sure whether (3) is supposed to mean the same as (1) and (2), or to mean rather that Smith single-handed can outplay the whole team in a body. This latter sense has little to do with (1) and (2), and indeed involves no quantification at all; it could be phrased simply 'Smith can outplay the team'.

Commonly it is possible also to use 'each' or 'any' instead of 'every'. Thus §34(3) may be read 'Each thing is itself', 'Anything is itself'. Likewise (1) may be rephrased:

(4)   Smith can outplay each member of the team,

(5)   Smith can outplay any member of the team.

But it is important to note that these versions differ radically in their behavior under denial. If we attach 'not' to 'can' in (1), we get a genuine denial of the whole. The statement 'Smith cannot outplay every member of the team' expresses the denial of (2), i.e.:

(6) $(\exists x)(x$ is a member of the team $\cdot \sim$ Smith can outplay $x)$;

it amounts to saying that there is a member of the team (at least one) whom Smith cannot outplay. The case of (4) is similar. Attachment of 'not' to 'can' in (5), on the other hand, yields something quite different; the statement 'Smith cannot outplay any member of the team' is not really the denial of (5), for it amounts not to (6) but to:

$\sim(\exists x)(x$ is a member of the team $\cdot$ Smith can outplay $x)$

(cf. §33). This anomaly is typical of the reasons why logical symbols are useful.

It is often possible simply to omit 'every', or to switch to the plural form as above and omit 'all', without changing the meaning. Thus the statement:

(7) $\sim(\exists x)(x$ is a man $\cdot \sim x$ is mortal)

might be phrased simply 'Man is mortal', or 'Men are mortal'—as well as 'Every man is mortal', 'All men are mortal'. Similarly §34(7) might be phrased simply 'Outdoor sports bore George'. There are cases, however, where statements constructed thus without any synonym of 'every' or 'all' carry quite other senses. E.g., whereas 'Man is mortal' means that each man is mortal, 'Man has waged war from time immemorial' does not mean that each man has waged war from time immemorial; nor does 'Man is a species' mean that each man is a species. Again, whereas 'Men are mortal' means that each man is mortal, 'Men are numerous' does not mean that each man is numerous.

Often also the sense of 'every' is carried simply by 'a'—even though 'a' often carries rather the sense of 'some'. This pair of usages was commented upon earlier (§32). Another variation is the use of 'what' or 'whatever' in place of 'everything that'; thus §34(4) may be shortened to read 'Whatever interests me bores George'.

Since a statement such as (2), (7), §34(3), §34(6)–(7), etc. begins with '$\sim(\exists x)$', all the verbal versions generally available for statements of the latter kind (§33) carry over and provide further alternatives to the 'every' idiom. E.g., since §34(3) consists in effect of '$\sim(\exists x)$' applied to 'x is not itself', it may be read 'Nothing is not itself'. Again (2) might be read 'There is no member of the team that Smith cannot outplay'.

Additional alternatives to 'every' arise from the fact that 'nothing that is not' commonly gives way to one or another idiom involving 'nothing but' or 'only', as in 'Nothing but what bores George interests me', 'Only that which bores George interests me'. These amount to 'Nothing that does not bore George interests me', and hence go into symbols according to §33 as:

$$\sim(\exists x)(\sim x \text{ bores George . } x \text{ interests me}),$$

i.e., §34(6).

A further way of reading (2), (7), §34(6)–(7), and their like is to be found in §8; for these statements amount precisely to *general conditionals*. This is seen—in the case, e.g., of §34(6)—by inserting '$\sim\sim$' in the fashion:

(8) $\sim(\exists x)\sim\sim(x \text{ interests me . } \sim x \text{ bores George})$;

for '$\sim(\exists x)\sim$' here can be read 'no matter what x may be' (cf. §34), and its sequel can be read 'if x interests me, then x bores George' (cf. §7). Thus (8) amounts to §8(2), and may be read 'If anything interests me it bores George'. More elaborate cases may be got by restricting the 'anything', in such contexts, by one or another of the usual devices (§34); e.g.:

(9)   If any movie interests me it bores George.

Symbolically, the restrictive clause is inserted conjunctively as usual:

(10) $\sim(\exists x)(x \text{ is a movie . } x \text{ interests me . } \sim x \text{ bores George})$.

Exercises

1. In view of the present section, how many further versions of (7) can you add to those in the preceding exercise?

2. In the statement:

> An orthodox Shiah regards a descendant of Ali as the true Caliph,

would you construe both 'an' and 'a' in the sense of 'every'? or both in the sense of 'some'? or one in the one sense and one in the other? How would you translate the whole into symbols?

§ 36. Persons

According to §34, restriction of 'everything' may be accomplished either by putting an appropriate substantive for 'thing' or by adding a relative clause. In giving §35(2) the reading §35(1), we used the first of these methods. Under the second method, on the other hand, §35(2) would be read:

Smith can outplay everything that is a member of the team,

or briefly:

Smith can outplay everything on the team.

But the grotesqueness of this result reminds us that standard English usage requires use of 'one' or 'body' or 'person' instead of 'thing' when only persons are relevant:

(1)   Smith can outplay everyone on the team.

'Thing' must be supplanted in this way not only in the context 'everything', and the variant contexts 'anything', 'each thing', but likewise in the contexts 'something' and 'nothing'; and any associated 'it' must of course be changed to 'he', and 'which' to 'who' or 'whom'. Correspondingly 'whatever' becomes 'whoever' or 'whomever':

(2)   Whoever interests me bores George.

Various of these personal usages, like the corresponding impersonal ones, can be switched over to the plural without change of meaning. The plurals of 'everyone' and 'someone' are simply 'all' and 'some', used as substantives.

The 'one' or 'body' of 'everyone' or 'everybody' is to be construed as 'person' and handled precisely as we handle any other restrictive substantive which may appear in place of the 'thing' of 'everything' (§34). Thus (2), in other words:

(3)   Everyone who interests me bores George,

goes into symbols not as §34(6) but as:

(4) $\sim(\exists x)(x$ is a person . x interests me . $\sim x$ bores George).

Analogous treatment applies where we have 'some' or 'no' in place of 'every'. Thus 'Somebody irritates me' becomes:

$(\exists x)(x$ is a person . x irritates me$)$;

again 'Someone in the town irritates me' becomes:

$(\exists x)(x$ is a person . x is in the town . x irritates me$)$.

Reëxamining (1) now in the light of these considerations, we see that it is not strictly translatable into §35(2), but rather into:

(5) $\sim(\exists x)(x$ is a person . x is on the team .

$\sim$ Smith can outplay $x)$.

In practice, of course, one would regard the clause 'x is a person' in (5) as redundant, since any member of the team is surely a person; and thus in practice the translation (5) of (1) does reduce to §35(2). Nevertheless it must be borne in mind that this redundancy is not purely logical; logically the status of 'x is a person' in (5) is the same as in (4). Logic alone does not tell us that only persons are on the team, any more than it tells us that only persons interest me.

We can still conveniently drop 'x is a person', even from (4), by viewing 'x' as *intrinsically* limited to persons for the space of a given discussion. '$(\exists x)$' means 'there is an entity x such that'; and there is no logical objection to conceiving of this universe of 'entities', for purposes of '$(\exists x)$', as comprising persons only. But in practicing this dodge we must take care lest there be other places in the same discussion where we want our variables to range over additional entities.

Exercise

Put into symbols, with and without explicit personal restriction:

I see nobody more often than Arthur, nor is there anyone whom I am less disposed to see.

§ 37. Times and Places

Just as the 'thing' of 'something', 'nothing', and 'everything' (or 'anything') is commonly restricted to *persons* by substituting 'one' (cf. §36), so it is commonly restricted to *places* by substituting 'where'. Restriction to *times* or dates is accomplished by changing 'something' to 'sometime' or 'sometimes' or 'once', and changing 'nothing' and 'everything' to 'never' and 'always'. Associated occurrences of 'it' give way to 'there' for place and 'then' for time, and associated occurrences of 'which' give way to 'where' for place and 'when' for time. Correspondingly 'whatever' becomes 'wherever' or 'whenever', or, elliptically, 'where' or 'when'.

Thus these idioms involve no special problem. If a statement involves any of the words 'somewhere', 'sometime', 'nowhere', 'never', 'everywhere', 'always', its translation into symbols is effected simply by expanding the word in question into 'at some place', 'at some time', 'at no place', 'at no time', 'at every place', or 'at every time', and then proceeding along the lines of earlier sections. 'Jones is never ill', e.g., becomes 'Jones is ill at no time'; and this goes into:

$$\sim(\exists x)(x \text{ is a time . Jones is ill at } x)$$

precisely as 'Boston is far from no city' went into §33(5).

But there are subtleties to look out for. The statement:

(1)   Tai always eats with chopsticks

would seem to become 'Tai eats with chopsticks at all times', which goes into:

(2) $\sim(\exists x)(x \text{ is a time . } \sim \text{ Tai eats with chopsticks at } x)$

just as §35(3) goes into §35(2). However, this translation construes (1) as meaning that Tai is *always* eating and using chopsticks in the process; whereas (1) is more likely to mean merely 'Whenever Tai eats he uses chopsticks', i.e. 'At every time at which Tai eats he uses chopsticks', i.e.:

(3) $\sim(\exists x)(x \text{ is a time . Tai eats at } x \text{ . } \sim \text{ Tai uses chopsticks at } x).$

(3) suggests daintiness, (2) gluttony.

Here, then, is another example of the difficulty of establishing a mechanical routine for translating words into symbols. An understanding of the ambiguous statements of ordinary language calls for sympathetic reading and an element of implicit psychologizing; and these are essential factors in translating words into rigorous symbolism. One utility of the symbols is in recording unambiguously the decision to which our sympathetic reading and psychologizing have led.

Frequently 'sometimes', 'always', and 'never' are used where actually no reference to time is intended; e.g. 'Squares of odd numbers are always odd', 'Squares of odd numbers are never even'. In such cases the 'sometimes', 'always', and 'never' function simply as transplanted occurrences of 'some', 'all', and 'no'. Thus the two examples at hand could be rephrased in more straightforward fashion as 'All squares of odd numbers are odd' and 'No squares of odd numbers are even'.

Far more frequently, on the other hand, a really essential reference to time is left tacit. It has been remarked (§2) that statements are to be thought of strictly as involving tenseless verbs, and that all temporal limitations which might ordinarily be indicated by tense or tacitly understood are to be thought of strictly as introduced by explicit references to dates or periods. But we agreed, for the sake of natural and simple examples, to waive this demand in practice and merely pretend that it is fulfilled. It should be noted, however, that the references to time which are thus left unanalyzed are commonly of a kind which would demand additional quantification if made explicit. The statement:

(4)   Olaf has seen Stromboli, but it was not erupting,

e.g., remains essentially unanalyzed if merely represented as:

Olaf has seen Stromboli . $\sim$ Stromboli was erupting

without regard to the temporal factor; for one's natural intention in affirming (4) is to bring out the simultaneity of Olaf's seeing Stromboli with Stromboli's failure to erupt. This would be expressed quantificationally, and tenselessly, by saying that there is some one time at which Stromboli is both being seen by Olaf and failing to erupt:

$(\exists x)(x$ is a time . Olaf sees Stromboli at x . $\sim$ Stromboli erupts at x).

If we want to indicate further that that time is past, i.e. prior to September 14, 1940, there is no difficulty in doing so:

(5) $(\exists x)(x$ is prior to Sept. 14, 1940 .
           Olaf sees Stromboli at x . $\sim$ Stromboli erupts at x).

Exercise

Put these into symbols:

When it rains in Pago Pago it pours.

I never go anywhere by train if I can get there by plane.

§ 38. Quantification in Context

Confronted with the problem of paraphrasing a complicated verbal statement into the symbolism of quantification, conjunction, and denial, we must consider how the intended meaning of each of its constituent idioms could be expressed in terms of the symbols. The numerous forms dealt with in foregoing sections provide *examples* of this process, and the reader should study them as examples rather than depend on them as a dictionary.

It will be instructive to start with an unusually difficult case:

(1)   Once a salesman sells a radio to a man who hates radios, he has mastered his trade.

The 'once' here is a means of indicating that the salesman has mastered his trade by the time of the sale, rather than at some later time. Moreover, it is obviously intended that the man hate radios at the time of the sale, rather than merely at some earlier or later time. We can make these temporal matters explicit by rephrasing (1) thus:

> If at any time a salesman sells a radio to a man who hates radios at that time, he masters his trade by that time,

where the verbs are construed tenselessly. Analogously to the translation of §35(5) into §35(2), this becomes:

(2) $\sim(\exists x)(x$ is a time . $\sim$ if at x a salesman sells a radio to a man who hates radios at x, he masters his trade by x).

We have next to deal with the part:

(3)   if at x a salesman sells a radio to a man who hates radios at x, he masters his trade by x.

Clearly this is supposed to hold regardless of the salesman; the 'a' of 'a salesman' may be read 'any'. Accordingly (3) becomes:

> $\sim(\exists y)(y$ is a salesman . y sells a radio at x to a man who hates radios at x . $\sim y$ masters y's trade by x).

Putting this for (3) in (2), and cancelling '$\sim\sim$', we have:

(4)   ~($\exists x$)(x is a time . ($\exists y$)(y is a salesman . y sells a radio
        at x to a man who hates radios at x . ~ y masters y's
        trade by x)).

We have next to deal with the part:

(5) y sells a radio at x to a man who hates radios at x.

Clearly this means merely that y sells the man some radio, not every
radio; 'a radio' here thus has the sense of 'some radio'. Just as 'I
wrote a poem' became §32(3), then, (5) becomes:

> ($\exists z$)(z is a radio . y sells z at x to a man who hates radios
> at x).

Thus (4) becomes:

(6)   ~($\exists x$)(x is a time . ($\exists y$)(y is a salesman . ($\exists z$)(z is a radio .
        y sells z at x to a man who hates radios at x) . ~ y
        masters y's trade by x)).

We have yet to deal with the part:

> y sells z at x to a man who hates radios at x.

Clearly 'a' here is again 'some'; so we get:

> ($\exists w$)(w is a man . w hates radios at x . y sells z at x to w).

Thus (6) becomes:

(7)   ~($\exists x$)(x is a time . ($\exists y$)(y is a salesman . ($\exists z$)(z is a radio
        . ($\exists w$)(w is a man . w hates radios at x . y sells z at x to
        w)) . ~ y masters y's trade by x)).

Finally 'w hates radios at x' is obviously intended in the sense 'w
hates all radios at x', and thus becomes:

> ~($\exists v$)(v is a radio . ~ w hates v at x).

So (7) as a whole becomes:

(8)   ~($\exists x$)(x is a time . ($\exists y$)(y is a salesman . ($\exists z$)(z is a radio
        . ($\exists w$)(w is a man . ~ ($\exists v$)(v is a radio . ~ w hates v at
        x) . y sells z at x to w)) . ~ y masters y's trade by x)).

Comparison of (1) with (8) shows that everyday language has certain virtues as a practical medium. Only on translating (1) into (8),
however, do we succeed in exposing the logical structure of (1) and
opening the way to general rules for the manipulation of (1) and
related statements. Such rules will be formulated in Chapter IV; but

a major step of analysis is already achieved in getting from (1) to
(8).

Since we cannot safely undertake to analyze so complex a statement as (1) in a single step, it is advisable to attend to one idiom at a
time as in the above steps. Moreover, it is advisable, as above, to
take cognizance of the most *outward* structure first and work in-
ward step by step; this plan helps avoid confusions of grouping,
just as was noted (§13) in connection with statement composition.
The importance also of two further cautions is apparent from the
above example: (a) choose a new variable for each new quantifier,
and (b) take care to repeat that variable in all and only those subsequent positions where a reference back to this quantifier suits the
intended meaning.

When occasion arises for paraphrasing verbal connectives in the
midst of quantifiers, we need also to supplement the canon at the
end of §13 with this analogue: on paraphrasing a verbal segment
into a symbolic conjunction, enclose the conjunction in parentheses
in case it is immediately preceded by a quantifier.

Exercises

1. Put these into symbols step by step, using two quantifiers in
each:

> Nobody in this room is heavier than everyone in the next.

> Whoever contributes something to the fund gains our undy-
> ing gratitude.

2. Put this into symbols step by step, using three quantifiers corresponding to 'when', 'a', 'a':

> When a male Eskimo comes of age he is presented with a
> harpoon by the patriarch of his village.

Hint: First stage, analogous to (2):

> $\sim(\exists x)(x$ is a time . $\sim$ a male Eskimo who comes of age at x
> is presented at x with etc.).

Second stage, analogous to (4):

> $\sim(\exists x)(x$ is a time . $(\exists y)(y$ is male etc. . $\sim y$ is presented
> etc.)).

Alternative approach, first stage:

$\sim(\exists x)(x$ is male . x is an Eskimo . $\sim$ when x comes etc.).

3. Put this into symbols, using five quantifiers, whereof three have to do with time, one with boys, and one with deeds:

A boy is a Boy Scout in good standing only if he has been duly admitted and has done a good deed every day thenceforward.

Hint: He is in good standing at any time only if he was admitted at an earlier time and did a good deed every day meanwhile.

IV • QUANTIFICATIONAL INFERENCE

§ 39. Quantificational Schemata

WHEREAS SCHEMATA built up of statement letters sufficed to exhibit the forms of statements in point of statement composition, an elaboration of the statement letter becomes necessary when we turn our attention to quantification. We have now to provide for the representation not only of component statements but also of component open sentences. In representing an open sentence we must preserve a record of any variables therein that may refer back to quantifiers elsewhere in the context, for these contribute essentially to the logical structure of the whole.

Accordingly, just as 'p', 'q', etc. are used in place of statements, so 'Fx', 'Gx', 'Hx', 'Fy', 'Gy', 'Fxy', 'Gxy', '$Fxyz$', etc. will be used in place of open sentences. We call 'F', 'G', etc. *predicate letters*. These, like statement letters (§30), are schematic: they are incapable of occurring in sentences, as variables do.

Let us call 'Fx', 'Fy', 'Gx', 'Gy', 'Fxy', 'Gxx', '$Fxyz$', etc. *atomic open schemata*. Thus an atomic open schema consists of a predicate letter and a string of (one or more) variables, with or without repetitions. Let us refer to statement letters and atomic open schemata collectively as *atomic schemata*. Now the atomic schemata, together with all expressions thence constructible by truth functions and quantification, are called *quantificational schemata*. The previous notion of schema, more explicitly *truth-functional* schema (§14), is thereby extended; quantificational schemata comprise all the truth-functional schemata plus the atomic open schemata plus such further expressions as:

(1) $(\exists x)Fx$, $(\exists x)Fxy$, $(\exists x)p$, $(\exists y)(\exists x){\sim}Fxy$,

$(\exists x)(p \cdot Fx)$, ${\sim}(\exists x)(Fx \cdot Fy)$, ${\sim}(\exists x)(Fx \cdot Gxy)$,

$(\exists y){\sim}(\exists x)(Fx \cdot Gy)$, ${\sim}(q \cdot (\exists y){\sim}(\exists x){\sim}(Fx \cdot Gxy))$.

But the following restriction is to be observed in building quantificational schemata: *no one predicate letter can carry strings of variables of different lengths within the same schema.* In view of this we cannot use 'Fx' in the same schema with 'Fxx', 'Fxy', 'Fyz', 'Fxyz', etc., nor can we use 'Fxyz' in the same schema with 'Fx', 'Fxx', 'Fxy', 'Fyz', etc. On the other hand we can use 'Fx' in the same schema with 'Fy', 'Gxy', 'Hxyz', etc.; likewise we can use 'Fxy' in the same schema with 'Fyz', 'Fxx', 'Gx', 'Hxyz', etc.

An occurrence of a variable in a quantifier is said to be *bound*. All recurrences of the variable, in the sentence or schema governed by that quantifier, are likewise said to be bound. Occurrences of a variable that are not bound are called *free;* and the variable is said to be free in a given expression if it has a free occurrence in the expression. Thus 'x' is free in the open sentence §30(1), and 'y' in §30(2), and both 'x' and 'y' in §30(3); on the other hand 'x' is not free in §30(2). Again 'y' is free in the second, sixth, and seventh of the schemata listed in (1) above.

The difference between a statement and an open sentence is simply that an open sentence has one or more free variables while a statement has none. Correspondingly, quantification schemata are *open* or *closed* according as they do or do not have free variables. Thus the second, sixth, and seventh of the schemata in (1) are open and the other six are closed. All truth-functional schemata are closed schemata, for they have no variables at all.

Exercise

Which of the following are quantificational schemata? Which are truth-functional schemata? Which are closed?

$$p \cdot \sim(q \cdot \sim p),$$
$$Fx \cdot \sim(Gxy \cdot \sim Fx),$$
$$Fx \cdot \sim(\exists y)(Gxy \cdot \sim Fx),$$
$$Fx \cdot \sim(\exists x)(Gxy \cdot \sim Fx),$$
$$(\exists x)Fx \cdot \sim(\exists x)(Gxy \cdot \sim Fx),$$
$$(\exists x)\sim(\exists y)Fyz \cdot \sim(\exists x)(Gxy \cdot \sim Fx),$$
$$(\exists x)Fx \cdot \sim(\exists x)(\exists y)Gxy \cdot \sim Fy,$$
$$(\exists x)Fx \cdot \sim(\exists y)((\exists x)Gxy \cdot \sim Fy).$$

§ 40. Predicates

The notion of substitution hitherto dealt with (§14) was limited to substitution for statement letters in truth-functional schemata. But now predicate letters have taken a place alongside statement letters, and truth-functional schemata have been embedded in the broader category of quantificational schemata. A corresponding extension of the notion of substitution is called for, which will provide in general for substitution for statement and predicate letters in quantificational schemata.

In preparation for this general notion of substitution, it will be convenient to introduce the auxiliary device of *predicates*. Predicates are expressions formed from sentences by putting circled numerals for free variables. (Circled numerals are not supposed to mean anything, but they will be found useful in connection with substitution.) In particular it is convenient to allow the number of variables supplanted by circled numerals to be zero; thus a statement or open sentence is counted as a predicate too.

Correspondingly, the result of putting circled numerals for free variables in a schema will be called a *predicate-schema*.

The original notion of substitution was explained in terms of *introduction* of statements or truth-functional schemata at occurrences of statement letters. In preparation for the extended notion of substitution we must extend the notion of introduction, so as to be able to speak of introduction of predicates and predicate-schemata at occurrences of statement *or predicate* letters.

Introduction of a predicate or predicate-schema P at a given occurrence of a predicate letter consists in supplanting that occurrence and the attached string of variables (cf. §39) by the expression which we get from P by putting the initial variable of the string for '①', the next variable for '②', and so on. E.g., introduction of the predicate:

(1) $(\exists v)(⑤$ owes ② to ④ for v . $\sim$ ① paid ② to ④ for $v)$

at the second occurrence of 'G' in:

(2) $(\exists z)(Gxwyzy . \sim Gywwzx)$

yields:

(3) $(\exists z)(Gxwyzy$.

   $\sim(\exists v)$ (x owes w to z for v . $\sim y$ paid w to z for v));

we supplant '$Gywwzx$' as a whole by the open sentence which we get from (1) by putting 'y' for '①', 'w' for '②', 'w' again for '③' (this step happens to be vacuous, since '③' does not appear), 'z' for '④', and 'x' for '⑤'. Introduction of (1) at the *first* occurrence of 'G' in (2), on the other hand, yields rather:

(4) $(\exists z)((\exists v)(y$ owes w to z for v . $\sim x$ paid w to z for $v)$.
   $\sim Gywwzx).$

Introduction of the predicate-schema:

(5) $F①y③$. $(\exists v)Gv③$

at the second occurrence of 'G' in (2), again, yields:

(6) $(\exists z)(Gxwyzy$. $\sim(Fyyw$. $(\exists v)Gvw))$;

here we have supplanted '$Gywwzx$' by the schema which we get from (5) by putting 'y' for '①', 'w' for '②' (vacuous), 'w' again for '③', 'z' for '④' (vacuous), and 'x' for '⑤' (vacuous).

In strictness the above formulation of introduction needs, of course, a stipulation regarding parentheses: if the expression to be put for a letter is a conjunction or alternation, usually it must first be enclosed in parentheses.

Introduction of the predicate (1) at the occurrence of 'F' in the schema:

$$\sim(\exists z)(\exists x)\sim(\exists w)(\exists y)Fywuzx$$

yields the statement:

$\sim(\exists z)(\exists x)\sim(\exists w)(\exists y)(\exists v)(x$ owes w to z for v . $\sim y$ paid w to z for v).

Introduction of (1) at the occurrence of 'F' in the schema:

$$(\exists w)\sim(\exists y)Fywuzx$$

yields the open sentence:

$(\exists w)\sim(\exists y)(\exists v)(x$ owes w to z for v . $\sim y$ paid w to z for v).

Introduction of (5) at the second occurrence of 'F' in the schema:

$$(\exists z)(Fxzw$. $\sim Fywz)$$

yields the schema:

$$(\exists z)(Fxzw$. $\sim(Fyyz$. $(\exists v)Gvz)).$$

100

Analogously to what was noted in §14, the result of introduction may be a hybrid involving both schemata and words; witness (3) and (4). The result (6) is deviant on another count: it violates the restriction in §39. In some other cases, the result of introduction will retain circled numerals; e.g., introduction of (1) at the occurrence of 'G' in '$(\exists x)(p \cdot Gxy)$' yields:

$$(\exists x)(p \cdot (\exists v)(\text{⑤ owes } y \text{ to ④ for } v \cdot \sim x \text{ paid } y \text{ to ④ for } v)).$$

For statement letters the explanation of introduction is essentially the same as in §14. Introduction of S at an occurrence of a statement letter consists merely in putting S for that occurrence, first supplying any necessary parentheses. Introduction of the open sentence 'y prefers z to w' (a predicate lacking circled numerals) at the occurrence of 'p' in '$(\exists x)(p \cdot Gxy)$' yields simply:

$$(\exists x)(y \text{ prefers } z \text{ to } w \cdot Gxy).$$

Exercises

1. Write the result of introducing (1) at the first occurrence of 'F' in:

$$\sim Fxyz \cdot (\exists w)(\sim Gywxzxz \cdot (\exists u)Fuwu);$$

also the result of introducing (1) at the second occurrence of 'F'; also the result of introducing (1) at the occurrence of 'G'. Repeat, using (5) instead of (1).

2. Give a predicate whose introduction at the occurrence of 'F' in:

$$(\exists z)(Gxwyzy \cdot Fwzyyu)$$

will yield (3).

§ 41. Restraints on Introducing

The foregoing formulation of the notion of introduction is actually somewhat broader than is desirable. Two restrictions will now be imposed, and the term 'introduction' will be reserved henceforth for just those cases where the restrictions are met. The first restriction is this: *if a predicate or predicate-schema, P, is to be introduced at an occurrence of a predicate letter, the adjoined string of variables must exhibit no variable which reappears in a quantifier of P.* The predicate:

(1)   (∃x) ① was given by the king of x to the queen of ②

is to be regarded as incapable of introduction at any occurrence of '*F*' having, e.g., the context '*Fwx*'. The reason for this restriction may be roughly indicated as follows. If the described introduction of (1) were permitted, it would consist, according to §40, in replacement of the occurrence of '*Fwx*' by:

(2)   (∃x) w was given by the king of x to the queen of x.

Whereas (1) amounts to the words:

(3)   ① was given by the king of something to the queen of ②,

(2) does *not* amount correspondingly to the words:

w was given by the king of something to the queen of x,

but rather to the words:

(4) w was given by the king of something to the queen thereof.

(2) does not say of w and x what (1) says of ① and ②; rather, (2) is of an essentially different form from (1), as comparison of (3) and (4) clearly reveals. This failure of parallelism would disrupt the projected theory of substitution, and accordingly we withhold the term 'introduction' from such cases.

The second restriction is as follows: *P cannot be introduced in any schema whose quantifiers exhibit free variables of P.* This restriction has much the same motivation as the other. The underlying situation may best be apprehended by comparing a number of simple cases of introduction. Introduction of the respective predicates:

(5) y loves ①, z loves ①, w loves ①

at the occurrence of '*F*' in '(∃x)*Fx*' yields the respective open sentences:

(∃x) y loves x,   (∃x) z loves x,   (∃x) w loves x,

in words 'y loves someone', 'z loves someone', 'w loves someone';[1]

---

[1] Or 'something'; cf. end of §36.

and introduction of '① loves ①' yields rather the statement '(∃x) x loves x', in words 'Someone loves himself'. This contrast between the result of introducing the predicate '① loves ①' and the results of introducing the predicates (5) is quite in keeping with the basic difference in form between the predicate '① loves ①' and the predicates (5). But now consider the introduction of 'x loves ①'. This, if it were allowed, would again yield '(∃x) x loves x'—despite the fact that 'x loves ①' is structurally analogous rather to the predicates (5) than to '① loves ①'. It is because of such anomalies that our second restriction is adopted, forbidding the introduction, e.g., of 'x loves ①' in '(∃x)Fx'. Introduction of a predicate at the occurrence of 'F' in '(∃x)Fx' is supposed to yield a quantification with respect to just those places which are marked '①' in the predicate; and whereas this end is achieved in the case of the predicates (5), and equally in the case of '① loves ①', it would not be achieved in the case of 'x loves ①'.

To sum up, then, introduction of a predicate P at a given occurrence of a letter L in a schema S is to be understood in the sense of §40 only in cases where no variable appearing in a quantifier of P appears in a string of variables attached to the given occurrence of L, and no variable appearing in a quantifier of S is free in P. Other cases are denied the status of introduction. A predicate or predicate-schema containing '(∃x)' cannot be introduced at an occurrence of a predicate letter followed by a string containing 'x', and a predicate or predicate-schema in which 'x' is free cannot be introduced in a schema containing '(∃x)'.

Introduction of sentences and sentence-schemata for statement letters can no longer go unrestricted either, now that variables and quantifiers are around. The second restriction above is needed no less where the predicate P is a sentence than elsewhere; and the reasoning is the same. Expressions are not to be introduced in schemata whose quantifiers exhibit free variables of the introduced expressions.

Exercises

1. Is there any predicate which can be introduced at the first occurrence of 'F' in the schema shown in Exercise 1, §40, and yet cannot be introduced at the second occurrence of 'F'? Is there any

predicate which can be introduced at the second occurrence of 'F' and not at the first? Is there any predicate which can be introduced at either occurrence of 'F' and yet not at the occurrence of 'G'? Is there any predicate which can be introduced at the occurrence of 'G' and yet at neither occurrence of 'F'? Justify your answers. In the case of each affirmative answer, give an example.

2. If §40(1) is to be capable of introduction at a given occurrence of a letter, what conditions must be met? Similarly for §40(5)?

§ 42. Substitution Extended

Now the general formulation of substitution can follow precisely the lines of the more special formulation in §14. *Substitution* of predicates or predicate-schemata for statement and predicate letters, in a quantificational schema S, consists in introducing the predicates or predicate-schemata at occurrences of the letters according to these rules: (a) *whatever is introduced at one occurrence of a letter is introduced also at all other occurrences of that letter throughout S*, and (b) *the final result is a statement or open sentence or quantificational schema.*

Thus substitution of the respective predicates:

(1)   (∃z) ① owes z to ②, w hates ①, y is rich

for 'F', 'G', and 'p' in the open schema:

(2) $\sim(∃x)(Fyx . \bar{p} . Gx . \sim Fxw)$

yields the open sentence:

(3) $\sim(∃x)((∃z)$ y owes z to $x . \sim y$ is rich .
                                        w hates $x . \sim(∃z)$ x owes z to w).

(3) is got from (2) by introducing '(∃z) ① owes z to ②' at *each* occurrence of 'F', 'w hates ①' at the occurrence of 'G', and 'y is rich' at the occurrence of 'p'. Introduction of '(∃z) ① owes z to ②' at the respective occurrences of 'F' consists in replacing 'Fyx' and 'Fxw' respectively by '(∃z) y owes z to x' and '(∃z) x owes z to w'; and introduction of 'w hates ①' at the occurrence of 'G' consists in replacing 'Gx' by 'w hates x'. Introduction of 'y is rich' at 'p' consists merely in putting 'y is rich' itself for 'p'.

Again, substitution of the respective predicates (1) for '*F*', '*G*', and '*p*' in the closed schema:

(4) $(\exists v)(\sim(\exists x)(Fvx \cdot Gx \cdot \bar{p}) \cdot (\exists u)Fvu)$

yields the open sentence:

(5) $(\exists v)(\sim(\exists x)((\exists z)$ *v* owes *z* to *x* $\cdot$ *w* hates *x* $\cdot$ $\sim$ *y* is rich) $\cdot$
$(\exists u)(\exists z)$ *v* owes *z* to *u*).

On the other hand, substitution of:

(6) $(\exists z)$ ① owes *z* to ②,   Smith hates ①,   Jones is rich

respectively for '*F*', '*G*', and '*p*' in the closed schema (4) yields rather the statement:

(7) $(\exists v)(\sim(\exists x)((\exists z)$ *v* owes *z* to *x* $\cdot$ Smith hates *x* $\cdot$ $\sim$ Jones is rich) $\cdot$ $(\exists u)(\exists z)$ *v* owes *z* to *u*).

Substitution of the respective predicate-schemata:

$$(\exists z)F①z②, \qquad Gw①, \qquad Hy$$

for '*F*', '*G*', and '*p*' in (4) yields the schema:

(8) $(\exists v)(\sim(\exists x)((\exists z)Fvzx \cdot Gwx \cdot \sim Hy) \cdot (\exists u)(\exists z)Fvzu)$.

The possibility of substitution is contingent, at each step, upon the possibility of introduction (cf. §41). Thus a predicate having '*x*' as a free variable cannot be substituted in a schema containing '$(\exists x)$'; nor can a predicate containing '$(\exists x)$' be substituted for a predicate letter which governs a string of variables containing '*x*'. However, there are no such obstacles in the foregoing examples.

Not only is the possibility of substitution contingent upon that of introduction, but it is contingent further on (b) above: the result must be a statement or open sentence or quantificational schema. This condition likewise is met in the foregoing examples; but there are various ways in which, in other cases, it might fail to be met. If predicates are introduced at some of the predicate and statement letters while other predicate or statement letters are left untouched, then the result will be a hybrid expression of the type §40(3)–(4). The same sort of result will arise if predicate-schemata are introduced at some places and predicates are introduced elsewhere. Again, if two of the introduced predicate-schemata exhibit the same predicate variable attached to strings of variables of different lengths, then the result will violate §39. This violation may likewise ensue if an introduced predicate-schema contains a predicate letter which reappears with a string of variables of different length somewhere in the schema within which the introduction is being made. Again, if a predicate is introduced which contains a numeral too high to be reached by the string of variables at hand, the surviving circled numeral will prevent the result from being a statement or open sentence or quantificational schema.

The general formulation of *joint substitution,* like that of ordinary substitution, follows the lines of §14. Joint substitution of predicates or predicate-schemata for statement or predicate letters, in two or more given quantificational schemata, consists in introducing the predicates or predicate-schemata at occurrences of the letters in all those given schemata according to these rules: (a′) *whatever is introduced at one occurrence of a letter is introduced also at all other occurrences of that letter throughout all the given schemata,* and (b′) *the final results are statements or open sentences or quantificational schemata.*

The notion of an *instance* of a truth-functional schema (§15) will now be extended to closed schemata generally: an instance of a closed schema is any statement which can be got from the schema by substitution. The statement (7), e.g., is an instance of the schema (4). The notion of *corresponding instances* (§15) carries over in similar fashion. The two principles noted in §15 in connection with truth-functional schemata clearly hold for all closed schemata: (i) if one is formed from another by substitution, then all instances of the former are instances of the latter, and (ii) if a pair of schemata is formed from another pair by joint substitution, then any corresponding instances of the former pair are corresponding instances of the latter pair.

Not every result of substitution in a closed schema is an instance; for substitution in a closed schema can yield an open sentence or a schema rather than a statement (cf. (5), (8)). If we are to get an instance we must substitute predicates, not predicate-schemata; and predicates, moreover, without free variables.

An instance of a closed schema exhibits, in place of each statement letter, a statement; and, in place of each atomic open schema (cf. §39), a statement or open sentence with no free variables beyond the ones in that atomic open schema. The instance (7) of (4), e.g., exhibits the statement 'Jones is rich' in place of the '*p*' of (4), the open sentence '(∃*z*) *v* owes *z* to *x*' (with '*v*' and '*x*' as sole free variables) in place of the '*Fvx*' of (4), the open sentence 'Smith

106

hates x' in place of the 'Gx' of (4), and the open sentence '($\exists z$) v owes z to u' in place of the 'Fvu' of (4).

Exercises

1. Write the result of substituting §41(1) for 'F' in:

$$\sim(\exists z)((\exists y)Fyzy \cdot \sim(\exists y)Fzyw),$$

and translate it into words. Whether the statement thus formed is true or false is a question not of logic but, as it happens, of history; still, what is your judgment as to its truth value?

2. Specify two predicate-schemata whose joint substitution for 'F' and 'G' in the respective schemata:

(i) $(\exists x)(\sim Gx \cdot (\exists y)Fxy)$, $\sim(\exists y)(Gy \cdot \sim(\exists z)(Gz \cdot Fyz))$

will yield the respective schemata:

$(\exists x)(\sim(\exists w)Gxwx \cdot (\exists y)(\exists w)(Fwy \cdot Gywx))$,

$\sim(\exists y)((\exists w)Gywy \cdot \sim(\exists z)((\exists w)Gzwz \cdot (\exists w)(Fwz \cdot Gzwy)))$.

3. The above schemata (i) have corresponding instances which admit of these verbal translations:

Someone disclosed the password to a nonmember,

To each member the password is disclosed by a member.

Specify the predicates whose joint substitution for 'F' and 'G' yields those instances.

§ 43. Validity Extended

On taking up quantification we allowed 'v' to lapse for a while. It was always a dispensable abbreviation; and dispensing with it even made things easier in a way, narrowing the choices that confront us in paraphrasing words into symbols. But 'v' will presently be useful again.

Duality, also confinement of denial, were reasons in §21 for introducing the redundant 'v' and writing '$\sim(\bar{p}\bar{q})$' as '$p \vee q$'. Now for related reasons it is customary to introduce a redundant notation for *universal quantification*, writing '$\sim(\exists x)\sim Fx$' as '$(x)Fx$' or '$(\forall x)Fx$'

(cf. §34). The quantifier '(∃x)' is then called *existential*, to distinguish.

Between universal and existential quantification on the one hand, and conjunction and alternation on the other, the parallel is close. Thus suppose *a*, *b*, *c*, . . . are all the things in the universe. Then '(x)Fx' amounts to the conjunction '*Fa . Fb . Fc* . . . . ', while '(∃x)Fx' amounts to the alternation '*Fa* v *Fb* v *Fc* v . . . '. For this reason, some logicians who write 'ʌ' for conjunction write 'ʌ$_x$' for '(x)' and 'V$_x$' for '(∃x)'.

So long as we were mainly concerned with such matters as the paraphrasing of words into symbols and the general theory of substitution and equivalence, the excess notations 'v' and '(x)' would have been less help than nuisance. But in the next developments, which culminate in a proof technique for quantification theory, we shall find 'v' useful and '(x)' as well.

Truth-functional schemata were called *valid* (§23) when all their instances were true. This definition can be accepted for quantificational schemata generally, insofar as they are closed. But what of open schemata? Their instances, if we extend the notion of instance so far, will be open sentences and so neither true nor false.

The key is the universal quantifier. We form the *universal closure* of an open schema by prefixing universal quantifiers '(x)', '(y)', etc. corresponding to all free variables present. Now *an open schema may be said to be valid when its universal closure is valid; and a closed schema is valid when all its instances are true.*

This open schema is valid:

$$(1) \qquad \sim((x)Fx . \sim Fy),$$

e.g., 'If everything has mass, *y* has mass.' For, its universal closure is valid:

$$(2) \qquad (y)\sim((x)Fx . \sim Fy).$$

A typical instance of this closed schema says, in effect, pick anything, *y*; if everything has mass, *y* has.

A truth-functional schema was *inconsistent* when its denial was valid. This formulation of the matter can be retained for quantificational schemata generally. So far as closed schemata are concerned, it amounts to saying again that an inconsistent schema is one whose instances are all false. But it does not declare an open schema inconsistent whenever its universal closure is inconsistent. The relevant closure here is rather the *existential closure*, formed by prefixing '(∃x)', '(∃y)', etc. corresponding to all free variables present.

For, trace it. An open schema '——' is inconsistent, we decided, if and only if '~(——)' is valid; but '~(——)' is valid if and only if its universal closure:

$$(x)(y) \; . \; . \; . \; \sim(\text{——})$$

is valid; but it amounts to:

$$\sim(\exists x)(\exists y) \; . \; . \; . \; (\text{——})$$

and so is valid if and only if this:

$$(\exists x)(\exists y) \; . \; . \; . \; (\text{——})$$

is inconsistent. Thus *an open schema is inconsistent when its existential closure is inconsistent; and a closed schema is inconsistent when all its instances are false.*

One inconsistent open schema, accordingly, is the schema:

$$(3) \hspace{4em} (x)Fx \; . \; \sim Fy$$

whose denial was the valid (1). One inconsistent closed schema is the existential closure:

$$(4) \hspace{4em} (\exists y)((x)Fx \; . \; \sim Fy)$$

of (3).

In §26 one schema was said to *imply* another when inconsistent with the other's denial. This formulation carries over to quantificational schemata generally. Thus, since (3) is inconsistent, '$(x)Fx$' implies 'Fy'.

Exercises

1. Rewrite the schemata in Exercises 1–2 of §42 as briefly as you can using universal quantifiers and alternation and no existential quantifiers or conjunction.

2. Similarly for the exercises of §§39–40.

§ 44. Equivalence Extended

Equivalence, we observed in §26, *is mutual implication.* Now that implication has been extended to quantificational schemata generally, this characterization serves as a definition of equivalence for quantificational schemata generally. When in particular the schemata are closed, equivalence so defined amounts still, as in §16, to saying that the schemata have no corresponding instances with unlike truth values; when they are open, however, there is no question of truth values of instances.

A simple example of equivalence of closed schemata is afforded by:

(1) $(\exists w)Fw$, $(\exists x)Fx$, $(\exists y)Fy$, $(\exists z)Fz$,

etc. All these, throughout the alphabet of variables, are of course equivalent to one another. Similarly for:

(2) $(w)Fw$, $(x)Fx$, $(y)Fy$, $(z)Fz$.

Again, the schemata:

(3) $(\exists x)Fx \cdot p$, $(\exists x)(Fx \cdot p)$

are equivalent. For, any corresponding instances of (3) will exhibit some statement, e.g. 'Socrates is mortal', in place of 'p'. If that statement is false, then '$(\exists x)Fx \cdot p$' is false regardless of 'F'; also '$Fx \cdot p$' is false for all x regardless of 'F', so that '$(\exists x)(Fx \cdot p)$' is false. If on the other hand the statement for 'p' is true, then '$Fx \cdot p$' will have, for each choice of x, the same truth value as 'Fx', and thus '$(\exists x)(Fx \cdot p)$' will agree in truth value with '$(\exists x)Fx$'; but so will '$(\exists x)Fx \cdot p$'. Thus, whatever statement we take for 'p' and whatever predicate for 'F', the two schemata in (3) will agree in truth value.

The schemata:

(4) $(\exists x)Fx \lor p$, $(\exists x)(Fx \lor p)$

are, like (3), equivalent. This can be established by cases, as (3) was. The argument is left to the reader.

The next equivalences come of our defining '(x)' as '$\sim(\exists x)\sim$'.

(5) $\sim(\exists x)Fx$, $(x)\sim Fx$.

(6) $\sim(x)Fx$, $(\exists x)\sim Fx$.

The equivalences (3) and (4) want rounding out now for universal quantification.

(7) $(x)Fx \cdot p$, $(x)(Fx \cdot p)$.

(8) $(x)Fx \lor p$, $(x)(Fx \lor p)$.

Actually these are implicit in (3)–(6). Here is the proof of (7):

$$(x)\sim\sim Fx \cdot p \qquad\qquad §16(4)$$
$$\sim(\exists x)\sim Fx \cdot p \qquad\qquad (5)$$

$$\sim((\exists x)\sim Fx \vee \bar{p}) \qquad \S21(14)$$
$$\sim(\exists x)(\sim Fx \vee \bar{p}) \qquad (4)$$
$$(x)\sim(\sim Fx \vee \bar{p}) \qquad (5)$$
$$(x)(Fx . p) \qquad \S21(14)$$

The proof of (8) is similar.

The notion of transformation, forward and backward, was developed in §19. As the above proof illustrates, it is as useful in application to quantificational schemata in general as it was in application to truth-functional ones. We saw in §§18–19 that if transformation by a pair of equivalent truth-functional schemata leads from one truth-functional schema to another, then these latter two are equivalent. This law can be established for quantificational schemata generally by a fairly parallel but more complex argument, which will be passed over here.[1]

Herbrand called the equivalences (3)–(8) *rules of passage*. If a quantification is an immediate component of conjunction, alternation, or denial, then forward transformation by one of (3)–(8) serves to bring the quantifier out to govern the whole conjunction or alternation or denial. Thus take §43(2). We transform it successively thus:

$$(y)\sim(x)(Fx . \sim Fy) \qquad (7)$$
$$(y)(\exists x)\sim(Fx . \sim Fy) \qquad (6)$$

In this way any quantificational schema can be transformed into a so-called *prenex* one: a schema all of whose quantifiers are lined up at the beginning, with each governing the whole of the schema from there on.

There is an apparent obstacle when the quantifier that we want to bring out, to cover a conjunction or alternation, contains a variable that is free in the other component of the conjunction or alternation. We could not transform '$(\exists x)Fx . Gx$' into '$(\exists x)(Fx . Gx)$'; this would depend on substituting 'Gx' for 'p' in (3) in violation of the restriction at the end of §41. What we can always do, however, is reletter the quantification by (1) or (2) so as to avoid the clash. We can transform '$(\exists x)Fx . Gx$' thus:

$$(\exists y)Fy . Gx \qquad (1)$$
$$(\exists y)(Fy . Gx) \qquad (3)$$

In general, to transform a schema into prenex form, we may best begin by relettering quantifications so that the letters in all quan-

[1] A proof of substantially this law occupies §18 of *Mathematical Logic*.

tifiers are distinct from the free variables of the schema and from one another. Then we proceed with the rules of passage.

Exercise

Transform the schema:

$$\sim(x)(\exists y)Fxy \ \mathbf{v} \sim((\exists y)(z)Fyz \cdot \sim(x)(z)Fxz)$$

into a prenex schema, showing all steps.

§ 45. Inconsistency Proofs

We noticed that '$(x)Fx$' implies 'Fy' (§43). To this particular implication and others that have the same form (merely using different variables, or some substitution for 'F') a special name is given: *universal instantiation*. We say thus that universal instantiation leads from '$(x)Fx$' or '$(y)Fy$' to 'Fx', 'Fy', and 'Fz', and from '$(y)(Gy \ \mathbf{v} \ Hz)$' to '$Gx \ \mathbf{v} \ Hz$', and from '$(z)Gzy$' to '$Gyy$', and so on. In general, universal instantiation consists in dropping an initial universal quantifier and perhaps supplanting the recurrences of the variable of that quantifier by another variable but not by one that already appears in further quantifiers.

This latter caution is wanted lest '$(\exists y)Gyy$', e.g., be called universal instantiation of '$(x)(\exists y)Gxy$'. For '$(x)(\exists y)Gxy$' and '$(\exists y)Gyy$' are not proper results of substitution in '$(x)Fx$' and 'Fy'; substitution of '$(\exists y)G(\textcircled{1})y$' for '$F$' in '$Fy$' would violate the first restriction in §41. '$(\exists y)Gyy$' is not implied by '$(x)(\exists y)Gxy$' on any account, universal instantiation or another; for if we put 'x is different from y' for 'Gxy', '$(x)(\exists y)Gxy$' becomes true and '$(\exists y)Gyy$' false.

Existential instantiation is the same operation as universal instantiation except that the quantifier is existential. Thus existential instantiation leads from '$(\exists x)Fx$' to 'Fz', and from '$(\exists y)(Gy \ \mathbf{v} \ Hz)$' to '$Gx \ \mathbf{v} \ Hz$', and so on. Unlike universal instantiation, existential instantiation does not assure implication; '$(\exists x)Fx$' does not imply 'Fz'. Still it has its uses. Thus suppose we are given some existential assumption, which I shall picture as '$(\exists x)(\text{---}x\text{---})$', and that we are reasoning from it. It tells us that there is at least one object fulfilling

112

'—x—'. Very well, we say, let z be such an object. If the letter 'z' is a fresh one, not already encumbered with other assumptions, there is no fallacy in adopting it thus as a nonce name for the assumed object. Such is existential instantiation. We proceed to reason from '—z—', which is more convenient than '$(\exists x)(—x—)$' in not having the quantifier. If finally we can derive an inconsistency, we have refuted the initial '$(\exists x)(—x—)$' itself.

We can illustrate this technique by proving the incompatibility of the statements:

There is someone who loves everyone,

There is someone whom no one loves.

They are:

(1) $(\exists x)(y)(x \text{ loves } y)$.

(2) $(\exists x)(y)\sim(y \text{ loves } x)$.

Let z, we say, be such a one as is said in (1) to exist. So

(3) $(y)(z \text{ loves } y)$.

And let w be such a one as is said in (2) to exist. So

(4) $(y)\sim(y \text{ loves } w)$.

But (3) implies by universal instantiation that z loves w, and (4) implies by universal instantiation that $\sim(z \text{ loves } w)$; so we have a contradiction.

There thus emerges a technique for proving the inconsistency of schemata. The above argument can be set up as a proof by existential and universal instantiation that the schemata:

(5) $(\exists x)(y)Fxy$,

(6) $(\exists x)(y)\sim Fyx$

are inconsistent with each other, i.e., that their conjunction is inconsistent.

Proof of inconsistency:

(7)	$(y)Fzy$	(5)
(8)	$(y)\sim Fyw$	(6)
	Fzw	(7)
	$\sim Fzw$	(8)

113

In the proofs in earlier pages the lines came one from another by equivalence transformations. It must be borne in mind that this is not true of our new inconsistency proofs. Here the lines come always by universal or existential instantiation, according as the line cited began with a universal or an existential quantifier. The proof ends when, as above, a truth-functional inconsistency has been accumulated.

Each step of existential instantiation is subject to the urgent rule that *the variable adopted be hitherto unused.* But for this rule we could prove the inconsistency of '$(\exists x)Fx$' with '$(\exists x)\sim Fx$' by deriving 'Fy' from the one and '$\sim Fy$' from the other. Or again we could prove the inconsistency of '$(\exists x)Gxy$' with '$(x)\sim Gxx$' by deriving 'Gyy' from the one and '$\sim Gyy$' from the other. Obviously '$(\exists x)Fx$' and '$(\exists x)\sim Fx$' are in fact consistent; take 'Fx' as 'x enjoys ballet' and both become true. Also '$(\exists x)Gxy$' and '$(x)\sim Gxx$' are consistent; take 'Gxy' again as 'x is different from y'.

The inconsistency that terminates an inconsistency proof is not always as overt as the 'Gyy' and '$\sim Gyy$', the 'Fy' and '$\sim Fy$', and the 'Fzw' and '$\sim Fzw$' of the foregoing examples, but it is always truth-functional. That is, an inconsistency proof ends up with a schema which is (or with several schemata whose conjunction is) simply an inconsistent truth-functional schema with atomic schemata like 'Fzw' in place of 'p', 'q', etc., and we know from §25 how to test for such inconsistency.

When an inconsistency proof is directed against two or more quantificational schemata, as in the case of (5) and (6) above, what it proves is the inconsistency of their conjunction. Also we may have an inconsistency proof of a single schema that is not outwardly a conjunction. Here is one.

(9) $(\exists x)(y)(z)(Fxy \cdot \sim Fzx)$

Proof of inconsistency:

(10) $(y)(z)(Fwy \cdot \sim Fzw)$ (9)

(11) $(z)(Fww \cdot \sim Fzw)$ (10)

        $Fww \cdot \sim Fww$ (11)

The method is suited to prenex schemata, taken singly as in the case of (9) or together as in the case of (5) and (6). But we know from §44 how to convert any quantificational schema into a prenex one. So our method of inconsistency proof is general.

And it constitutes a method for proving implication as well. To prove that '$(\exists x)(y)Fxy$' implies '$(y)(\exists x)Fxy$' (e.g., if there is someone who loves everyone, everyone is loved by someone or other), we would show (5) inconsistent with '$\sim(y)(\exists x)Fxy$', or, in prenex form, '$(\exists y)(x)\sim Fxy$', or, relettered, (6). We already did.

The method extends also to validity and equivalence; for a schema is valid if its denial is inconsistent, and schemata are equivalent if they imply each other.

The method can be shown to be *complete:* there is no inconsistent quantificational schema, nor (therefore) any inconsistent conjunction of quantificational schemata, that cannot be shown inconsistent by our method.[1] But the method is not a *test,* or *decision procedure.* It fails of that in that it gives verdicts only of inconsistency and not of consistency. In the face of persistent failure to arrive at an inconsistency proof for a given schema, there is in general no telling whether the schema is consistent or its inconsistency proof merely eludes us. For truth-functional schemata we do have a decision procedure (§25); it delivers an affirmative or negative answer to the inconsistency question every time. For quantificational schemata such a method is not only unknown but theoretically impossible.[2]

Exercises

1. Prove that these schemata are together inconsistent:

$$\sim(\exists x)Fx, \qquad (x)Gx, \qquad \sim(\exists x)(\sim Fx \cdot Gx).$$

2. Similarly for these:

$$(x)(Fx \cdot Gx), \qquad \sim((x)Fx \vee \sim(x)Gx).$$

3. Prove this schema inconsistent:

$$(\exists z)\sim(\exists x)(Fxxz \vee \sim(y)Fxyz).$$

[1] This was established by Kurt Gödel, "Die Vollständigkeit der Axiome des logischen Funktionenkalküls," *Monatshefte für Mathematik und Physik,* XXXVII (1930), 349–60, for a method of proof in quantification theory differing from ours. His argument can be adapted to our method, and even simplified in the application. See my *Methods of Logic,* Appendix.

[2] This has been established by Alonzo Church, "A Note on the Entscheidungsproblem," *Journal of Symbolic Logic,* I (1936), 40–41, 101–102.

4. In the light of the paragraph before last, prove these schemata equivalent:

$$(x)(Fx \cdot Gx), \qquad (x)Fx \cdot (x)Gx.$$

5. Similarly for these:

$$(\exists x)(Fx \vee Gx), \qquad (\exists x)Fx \vee (\exists x)Gx.$$

6. Prove what you can about the relations of these:

$$(x)(Fx \vee Gx), \qquad (x)Fx \vee (x)Gx,$$

$$(\exists x)(Fx \cdot Gx), \qquad (\exists x)Fx \cdot (\exists x)Gx.$$

§ 46. Logical Argument

Statements that were instances of valid or inconsistent truth-functional schemata were called truth-functionally true or false (§§24–25). More generally, now, statements that are instances of valid or inconsistent quantificational schemata at all may be called *quantificationally* true or false. The conjunction of §45(1) and §45(2) is quantificationally false. Similarly statements that are corresponding instances of equivalent quantificational schemata may be said to be quantificationally equivalent. When statements are corresponding instances of quantificational schemata one of which implies the other, the one may be said quantificationally to imply the other. Thus we see from the preceding section that 'There is someone who loves everyone' quantificationally implies 'Everyone is loved by someone or other'.

Logical truth itself, in the not quite determinate sense of page 1, could be identified with quantificational truth. Whether so to identify it is a question how broadly to take the category of "logical locutions". If we limit this to the sample list on page 1, then logical truth is quantificational truth and logical equivalence and implication are quantificational equivalence and implication. If on the other hand we reckon some locutions as logical that are not reducible to those, say '=' or even '∈' (§§47–48), then there will be logical truths and equivalences and implications that are not quantificational.

At any rate logic in the strictest sense is quantification theory, and a logical deduction in the strictest sense consists in establishing a quantificational implication. From one or more given statements, so-called premises, it may be claimed that a given statement follows logically as conclusion; and to substantiate this claim we show that the premiss or the conjunction of the premisses quantificationally implies the conclusion. We have seen how to show this. The process has several phases. First we paraphrase the desired conclusion and the premisses into terms of quantification, conjunction, alternation, and denial. Then we convert the premisses and the denial of the conclusion into prenex form (§44). Then we proceed with universal and existential instantiation, taking care in existential instantiation always to adopt new variables. When instantiation delivers lines without quantifiers, we scan or test them to see whether we have accumulated a truth-functional inconsistency, thus establishing the implication.

Suppose we are given the premisses:

(1)   The guard searched all who entered the premises except those who were accompanied by members of the firm,

(2)   Some of Fiorecchio's men entered the premises unaccompanied by anyone else,

(3)   The guard searched none of Fiorecchio's men,

and we want to show that the conclusion:

(4)   Some of Fiorecchio's men were members of the firm

follows. First we translate the premisses into symbols (cf. §38). (1) becomes successively:

$\sim(\exists x)(x$ entered the premises . $\sim x$ was accompanied by a member of the firm . $\sim$ the guard searched $x)$,

(5) $\sim(\exists x)(Ex . \sim(\exists y)(My . Ayx) . \sim Sx)$,

where 'Ex' abbreviates 'x entered the premises', 'My' abbreviates 'y was a member of the firm', 'Ayx' abbreviates 'y accompanied x', and 'Sx' abbreviates 'the guard searched x'. Similar translation of (2)–(4) yields:

(6) $(\exists x)(Fx . Ex . \sim(\exists y)(Ayx . \sim Fy))$,

(7) $\sim(\exists x)(Fx . Sx)$,

(8) $(\exists y)(Fy . My)$

where 'Fx' abbreviates 'x was one of Fiorecchio's men'.

Next we transform (5)–(7) progressively by §44(5)–(7) until they all end up in prenex form. These are the results:

(9) $(x)(\exists y)\sim(Ex . \sim(My . Ayx) . \sim Sx)$,

(10) $(\exists x)(y)(Fx . Ex . \sim(Ayx . \sim Fy))$,

(11) $(x)\sim(Fx . Sx)$.

Similarly the denial of the desired conclusion (8) goes over into the prenex form:

(12) $(y)\sim(Fy . My)$.

Then we start instantiating.

(13)	$(y)(Fw . Ew . \sim(Ayw . \sim Fy))$	(10)
(14)	$(\exists y)\sim(Ew . \sim(My . Ayw) . \sim Sw)$	(9)
(15)	$\sim(Ew . \sim(Mz . Azw) . \sim Sw)$	(14)
(16)	$Fw . Ew . \sim(Azw . \sim Fz)$	(13)
(17)	$\sim(Fw . Sw)$	(11)
(18)	$\sim(Fz . Mz)$	(12)

Here we stop, because (15)–(18) are together inconsistent. A general way of testing this is to put their conjunction into alternational normal form (§25). Actually it will be found that four preliminary steps of simplification by §20(5) reduce the conjunction of (15)–(17) to:

$$Mz . Azw . Fw . Ew . Fz . \sim Sw,$$

which already visibly contradicts (18).

Exercises

1. By the method of the present section, justify the following quantificational implications:

All the villagers admire Jasper. Either none of the villagers fear Jasper or some who fear him admire him.

All who flunk are lazy, but some students are neither bright nor lazy. Some students who are not bright do not flunk.

No policeman accepts bribes. No honest policeman accepts bribes.

Every generous man is esteemed by all who know him. If no one who is esteemed by all who know him need ever fear want, no generous man need ever fear want.

No one receives the *Bulletin* who has not paid his dues, and no member of the department has paid his dues. No member of the department receives the *Bulletin*.

2. Adhering to the same style, argue from 'Circles are figures' to 'Whoever draws a circle draws a figure'. (In the seventeenth century this was cited by Jungius as an inference inaccessible to syllogistic logic.)

3. Argue from the premisses:

Hector buys nothing from any natives except the Riffians,

Hector bought a fez from a blond native

to the conclusion 'Some Riffians are blond'.

4. Derive the same conclusion from the premisses:

The English buy nothing from any natives except the Riffians,

An English tourist bought a fez from a blond native.

5. Argue from the premisses:

The porter sees all who enter at the gate,

The porter never saw any of the defendants before this week

to the conclusion:

None of the defendants entered at the gate before this week.

Hint: The temporal emphasis in the second premiss and in the conclusion suggests that the temporal import also of the first premiss had better be made explicit on translation into symbols. Obviously the first premiss means that the porter sees all enterers when they enter.

§ 47. Identity and Singular Terms

No explicit mention has thus far been made of the simple sort of inference which leads from:

(1)   Tom married Sadie

to 'Someone married Sadie', i.e.:

(2) $(\exists x)\ x$ married Sadie.

119

Such inference can be accommodated under quantificational implication by letting a free variable play the role of the name. (1) and (2) can be depicted as 'Fz' and '$(\exists x)Fx$'. The required implication amounts then to the inconsistency of '$\sim(\exists x)Fx$' with 'Fz', and the proof is immediate:

$$Fz$$

$$(x)\sim Fx$$

$$\sim Fz$$

There was no occasion above to dislodge the name 'Sadie' in the manner of 'Tom', because of the fixity of the combination 'married Sadie' throughout the argument.

Our plan of representing names by free variables is defensible only when the name is a name of something in the range of our variables. Tom had better be in the range of the variable of quantification in (2), for he is the relevant value. This assumption—that the named object exists and is in the range of our variables—is best seen not as an added premiss, but as an assumption implicit in the act of paraphrasing the name as a free variable preparatory to formulating an argument.

Names are singular terms, but not all singular terms are names; not in the narrow sense. There are also complex singular terms like 'Sadie's husband', 'the coach at Bluffton', '$5 + 6$'. A general form under which all these can easily be brought is the form of *singular description,* 'the object x such that Fx', briefly '$(\imath x)Fx$'. What sets it off from simple names, for purposes of logical inference, is that there is logical structure inside it. We could use just 'z' for 'the coach at Bluffton' as well as for 'Tom' if all we wanted to deduce was (2) from:

The coach at Bluffton married Sadie.

But if we want to deduce that a coach married Sadie, we need to exploit the interior of 'the coach at Bluffton'. In general, where 'z' is made to stand for '$(\imath x)Fx$', we want to be able to declare among other things that Fz; the man who coaches at Bluffton coaches at Bluffton.

Also there is the matter of uniqueness. For the idiom '$(\imath x)Fx$', 'the object x such that Fx', is normally used only where we believe that there is one and only one object x such that Fx. Much of what goes into the condition 'Fx' is in practice left tacit, of course. Thus when we say 'the guard' we mean perhaps 'the man who was guarding the Argus offices on Easter morning, 1911'; and our use of the idiom indicates belief that there is only one such object, even though there are many objects x such that x is a guard. This sort of ellipsis is on a par with the elliptic usages noted in §2. Supposing the ellipsis filled in as part of 'Fx', then, the uniqueness condition that we want in general to be able to declare where 'z' stands for '$(\imath x)Fx$' is that

$$(3) \qquad \qquad {\sim}(\exists x)(Fx \,.\, {\sim}(x = z)),$$

i.e., Fx for nothing x but z. This and 'Fz' are two premisses whose adoption may conveniently be regarded as implicit in the act of letting 'z' stand for '$(\imath x)Fx$' in a quantificational argument. They will be called *descriptional premisses*. To show that a given conclusion follows from given premisses involving '$(\imath x)Fx$', we put some new free variable, say 'z', for '$(\imath x)Fx$' in premisses and conclusion and then prove that the conclusion thus modified is implied by the premisses thus modified *and* the descriptional premisses (3) and 'Fz'.

This way of handling singular descriptions keeps the description out of the formal argument; only a free 'z' appears for it. The descriptional notation '$(\imath x)Fx$' has no formal role except to prompt our recognition of the descriptional premisses (3) and 'Fz'. At the same time something new, not '$(\imath x)Fx$', does get into the formalism. It is the sign '$=$' of *identity* in (3). In general when we show that a conclusion follows from given premisses, including (3) and 'Fz', we do not use unaided quantification theory; to get all the good out of (3) we must invoke also the *axioms of identity*.

One axiom of identity is '$(x)(x = x)$'. The rest are the universal closures of the sentences and schemata that can be got by substituting for 'G' in this:

$$\sim(x = y \,.\, Gx \,.\, {\sim}Gy).$$

Such sentences are logically true if we count '$=$' as a logical locution, but they are not quantificationally true. Correspondingly for arguments involving singular descriptions: they establish logical implication out beyond quantificational implication.

Identity theory has uses in elementary logical reasoning also apart from singular descriptions. Thus suppose we want to argue from (1) and 'Sadie loved none but Tom' that

$$(4) \qquad {\sim}(\exists x)(\text{Sadie loved } x \,.\, {\sim}\, x \text{ married Sadie}).$$

'Sadie loved none but Tom' becomes, with 'z' for 'Tom',

(5) $\sim(\exists x)(\text{Sadie loved } x \cdot \sim(z = x))$.

So our problem is to show the denial:

(6) $(\exists x)(\text{Sadie loved } x \cdot \sim x \text{ married Sadie})$

of (4) inconsistent with (5) and 'z married Sadie'. The reader will find that he can carry this through by the method of §46 only if he supplements (5), (6), and 'z married Sadie' with one of the axioms of identity, viz.:

$(x)(y)\sim(x = y \cdot x \text{ married Sadie} \cdot \sim y \text{ married Sadie})$.

Exercises

1. Finish the problem of the last paragraph above.

2. Establish the conclusion:

> Some assessors have their wits about them

on the premisses:

> The assessor who was here yesterday got the better of our general manager,

> Anyone who gets the better of our general manager has his wits about him

and one descriptional premiss.

3. Establish the conclusion 'Barr is not the cashier' on the premisses 'Barr envies the cashier', 'Nobody envies himself', and, as axiom of identity, the closure of:

$\sim(x = y \cdot x \text{ envies } z \cdot \sim y \text{ envies } z)$.

§ 48. Membership

When we say that men are numerous, we mean neither that every man is numerous nor that some men are numerous. What is numerous is a certain abstract entity, the *class* of men. When we say that man is a zoological species, we mean that this abstract entity, the class of men, is a zoological species. When we say that the Apostles are twelve, or that they are a dozen, we mean again that an abstract entity, the *class* of Apostles, is a dozen; no Apostle is a dozen. Each Apostle is said to be a *member* of this abstract entity, the class of Apostles; and each man is said to be a member of the class of men. Symbolically, the form of notation '$x \epsilon y$' is used; thus Peter ϵ class of Apostles, and again Peter ϵ class of men.

The mathematics of membership or of classes, usually called *set theory*, has existence trouble. One would expect, given any open sentence in the role of 'Fx', that there be a class z such that

$$(x)(x \epsilon z \equiv Fx).$$

But this is too much to ask. Take 'Fx' as '$\sim(x \epsilon x)$' and you have *Russell's paradox:*

$$(x)(x \epsilon z \equiv \sim(x \epsilon x)).$$

The trouble with this is that it implies by universal instantiation the inconsistent sentence '$z \epsilon z \equiv \sim(z \epsilon z)$'.

The fundamental problem of set theory becomes that of settling what sentences, in the role of 'Fx', to assume a z for. Certain ones we must renounce outright, as seen. For the rest, we find that some may be assumed if others are not; and it is the quest for attractive combinations on this score that has made for the proliferation of distinct set theories.

One way of recovering part of the strength and convenience of the naïve law of class existence is by admitting some classes on the limited footing of *ultimate* classes: classes belonging to no further classes. The word 'set' is then reserved for the classes that are not ultimate. The idea of ultimate classes, due to von Neumann,[1] enables us consistently to revive the naïve law of class existence in this restricted form: given any condition on x, there does exist a class z—possibly ultimate, however—whose members are all and only the *sets* x meeting the condition. Then the question what classes are to exist reduces to the question what classes are to be sets. Here again there are many lines to choose among.

Besides its existence problems, a notable thing about the membership notion is its fecundity in definition. To begin with the least of

[1] J. von Neumann, "Eine Axiomatisierung der Mengenlehre," *Journal für reine und angewandte Mathematik,* CLIV (1925), 219–40. For a survey of various systems of set theory, see Part III of my *Set Theory and Its Logic* (Cambridge: Harvard University Press, 1963).

its definitional yield, there is '$x = y$'. Two ways of defining it suggest themselves. One, borrowing the abbreviation '$\equiv$' from §21, is:

(1) $(w)(w \,\epsilon\, x \equiv w \,\epsilon\, y)$,

i.e., x and y have the same members. The other is:

(2) $\sim(\exists z)(x \,\epsilon\, z \,.\, \sim(y \,\epsilon\, z))$;

for, if y belongs to every class z that x belongs to, then y belongs in particular to the class whose sole member is x. But (1) evidently falls short of '$x = y$' in cases where x and y are not classes; and (2) falls short in case x is an ultimate class. We may cover the ground by defining '$x = y$' rather as the conjunction of (1) and (2).

We can get much more. In combination with denial, conjunction, and quantification, the notion of membership is capable of serving all purposes which can be served by any of the notions of arithmetic, algebra, differential and integral calculus, or derivative branches of mathematics. Any theorem from any of these branches, e.g.:

$$5 + 11 = 16,$$

$$\sim(\exists x)(x \text{ is a number} \,.\, x \neq x + 0),$$

$$\sim(\exists x)(\exists y)(x \text{ is a number} \,.\, y \text{ is a number} \,.\, x + y \neq y + x),$$

can be translated into a statement (very long, to be sure) which is built up wholly of open sentences '$x \,\epsilon\, y$', '$x \,\epsilon\, z$', '$y \,\epsilon\, z$', etc., by means of denial, conjunction, and quantification.[1]

A celebrated theorem of Gödel says that no proof procedure can encompass all the truths of number theory, to the exclusion of falsehoods.[2] Since we can express number theory in set theory, it follows that there is no hope of a complete system of set theory. It is easy to show as a corollary that we cannot even complete the special department of set theory that comprises the assumptions of class existence, or of sethood.[3] So there can be no true minimizing of the exceptions to the naïve law of class existence. One can try only to minimize their obtrusiveness and inconvenience, and to achieve in one's axioms of class existence an attractive combination of strength and simplicity.

[1] Cf. *Mathematical Logic*, chap. III–VI.
[2] Kurt Gödel, "Ueber formal unentscheidbare Sätze der *Principia Mathematica* und verwandter Systeme," *Monatshefte für Mathematik und Physik*, XXXVIII (1931), 173–98.
[3] See p. 140 of my "Element and number," *Journal of Symbolic Logic*, VI (1941), 135–49.

Those who say that mathematics in general is reducible to logic are counting 'ϵ' in the vocabulary of logic and thus reckoning set theory to logic. This tendency has been encouraged by a confusion of the 'Fx' of logic with the '$x \epsilon z$' of set theory. Properly considered, 'F' is not a quantifiable variable referring to a class or attribute or anything of itself. The importance of this contrast between the schematic predicate letter 'F' and the quantifiable class variable 'z' is overwhelming, once we stop to consider what quantification over classes wrought. It compelled us, on pain of paradox, to recognize that some open sentences representable as 'Fx' were not representable as '$x \epsilon z$'. Even thus tamed, quantification over classes continued to produce discourse too comprehensive to be encompassed, as logic proper was, by a complete proof procedure. Also there is the difference of ontology: a statement expressed by quantifying over classes can depend for its truth on existence of special things—classes—while logical truths in the narrower sense treat of no one sort of thing as against another.

To say that mathematics in general has been reduced to logic hints of some new firming up of mathematics at its foundations. This is misleading. Set theory is less settled and more conjectural than the classical mathematical superstructure that can be founded upon it. These infirmities of set theory are themselves good reason to see set theory as an extralogical department of mathematics. Logic in the best and narrowest sense has all the firmness and dependability that its name connotes. Reality being what it is, we cannot expect most truths to admit of foundation purely within logic in such a sense.

INDEX

127